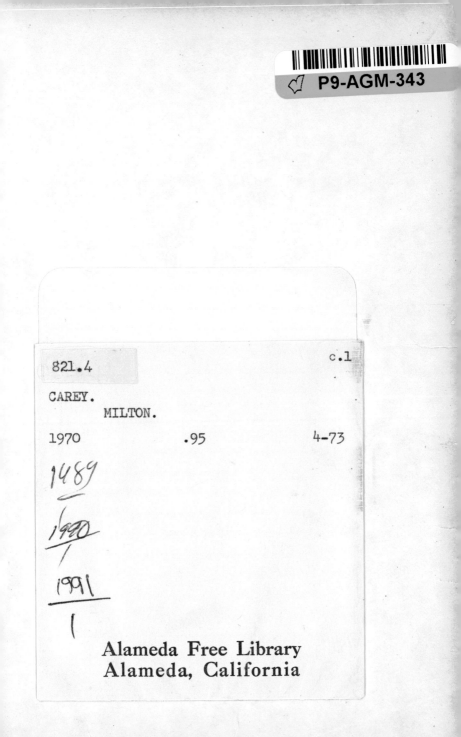

# ARCO
## Literary Critiques

# Milton

## John Carey, Ph.D.

arco
New York

Published 1970 by ARCO PUBLISHING COMPANY, Inc.
219 Park Avenue South, New York, N.Y. 10003
Copyright © John Carey, 1969, 1970
All Rights Reserved
Library of Congress Catalog Number 72-101770
Printed in the United States of America

# Arco Literary Critiques

Of recent years, the ordinary man who reads for pleasure has been gradually excluded from that great debate in which every intelligent reader of the classics takes part. There are two reasons for this: first, so much criticism floods from the world's presses that no one but a scholar living entirely among books can hope o read it all; and second, the critics and analysts, mostly academics, use a language that only their fellows in the same discipline can understand.

Consequently criticism, which should be as 'inevitable as breathing'—an activity for which we are all qualified—has become the private field of a few warring factions who shout their unintelligible battle cries to each other but make little communication to the common man.

*Arco Literary Critiques* aims at giving a straightforward account of literature and of writers—straightforward both in content and in language. Critical jargon is as far as possible avoided; any terms that must be used are explained simply; and the constant preoccupation of the authors of the Series is to be lucid.

It is our hope that each book will be easily understood, that it will adequately describe its subject without pretentiousness so that the intelligent reader who wants to know about Donne or Keats or Shakespeare will find enough in it to bring him up to date on critical estimates.

Even those who are well read, we believe, can benefit from a lucid exposition of what they may have taken for granted, and perhaps—dare it be said?—not fully understood.

K. H. G.

# Milton

Milton is an industry. The American and English presses pump out books and articles. The bibliographies fatten. There is even a *Milton Newsletter* (provenance: Athens, Ohio) to keep specialists up-to-the-minute. The enthusiasm could not be said to have permeated to the common reader. He has always found Milton remote, and now he is made to find him bewildering. Hence Milton's appropriateness as a *Literature in Perspective* subject. The scholarly colossus which keeps Milton from slipping (as Spenser has slipped) out of undergraduate and sixth-form syllabuses has a depressive effect on those for whom the syllabuses are designed. They are mistrustful, in its shade, about applying their own judgment to the poetry or to the moral and religious suppositions inherent in it. Perversely Milton, to whom orthodoxy was little more than the starting-point for dissent, has been made the preserve of orthodoxy himself. To provoke discussion around the fundamental issues with which he deals, as well as about the value of the verse he writes, should, I have assumed, be a primary concern of responsible Milton criticism.

Space is necessarily limited in books designed as a series. It has seemed best to me to use the area available discussing Milton's more important poems in as much detail as possible, instead of trying to mention every item in the canon. I have included, too, a short survey of his prose.

All quotations of Milton's poetry are from *John Milton, Complete Poems and Major Prose*, ed. Merritt Hughes, New York, 1957. The prose is quoted either from the (incomplete) *Complete Prose Works*, ed. Douglas Bush *et al.*, New Haven, 1953– , or from the *Works*, ed. F. A. Patterson *et al.*, New York, 1931–8 (these are abbreviated 'Yale' and 'Columbia' respectively). Other abbreviations are *PL* (*Paradise Lost*), *PR* (*Paradise Regained*) and *OED* (the *Oxford English Dictionary*).

I am very grateful to Kenneth Grose, the General Editor, for his friendly help and patience, as well as for occasional cries of protest.

J. C.

# Contents

# The Author

John Carey, M.A., D.Phil., is a Fellow in English Literature at St. John's College, Oxford. He has edited, with Alastair Fowler, *The Poems of John Milton* in the *Longmans' Annotated English Poets* series, and has translated Milton's *De Doctrina Christiana* for the Yale *Complete Prose Works*.

# Acknowledgements

The author and publishers are indebted to Yale University Press for permission to quote from *The Complete Prose Works of John Milton*, edited by Don M. Wolf, *et al*. The extracts from *John Milton, Complete Poems and Major Prose*, edited by Merritt Hughes, are reprinted with permission from The Odyssey Press. The extracts from *Works of John Milton, 1931–38* edited by F. A. Patterson, are reprinted with permission from Columbia University Press.

The cover portrait and the portrait of Milton at the age of twenty-one are reproduced by courtesy of the National Portrait Gallery. The manuscript of the draft of *Lycidas* is reproduced by courtesy of Trinity College Library, Cambridge; the portrait of John Milton at the age of ten is reproduced by courtesy of The Pierpont Morgan Library, New York; the portrait of Lady Alice Egerton at Cawdor Castle is reproduced by courtesy of the Right Honourable the Earl Cawdor.

The extract from *The Magic Mountain* by Thomas Mann, translated by H. T. Lowe-Porter, is reprinted with permission from Martin Secker & Warburg Ltd., and Alfred A. Knopf, Inc.

'I scarcely ever went from my lessons to bed before midnight': Milton in 1618

The author of the *Nativity Ode*: Milton at 21

The Lady of *Comus*

'With eager thought warbling his Doric lay': Milton's drafts for *Lycidas*
1–14 and 142–51

# I

# Portrait of the Artist

The bare bones of Milton's life can be laid out quickly enough. Born 1608, London; educated, St. Paul's School and Christ's College, Cambridge; then six years (1632–8) working at a programme of further education. This period produced *Comus* (1634) and *Lycidas* (1637). In 1638–9, fifteen months in Italy. Between 1641 and 1660, twenty-five prose tracts, mainly political, first joining the Puritan attack on the bishops of the Church of England; later defending the execution of Charles I (1649), as official spokesman for Cromwell's government, in the *Defence of the English People* (1651). Early in 1652, blindness. At the Restoration (1660), imprisonment for a few weeks in the Tower. In 1667, the publication of *Paradise Lost*; in 1671, that of *Paradise Regained* and *Samson Agonistes* (the latter possibly written twenty years earlier). In 1674, death.

But the bones do not help much. What would it have been like to know Milton? Not pleasant, is the general opinion. For a start, he was a Puritan: the word comes packed with notions of funereal suits and bigotry. Poets, if they must be religious, should at least be mystics. Everyone knows he ill-treated his first wife— else why should she have left him?—and that he made his daughters read him Hebrew and Greek without understanding it and did not even teach them to write. (Actually they had a governess, and their handwriting survives; but these are less familiar items.) And his erudition seems as inhuman as his misogyny: 'an appreciation of Milton is the last reward of consummated scholarship'. We are not encouraged to begin.

The popular image, like most, is not quite groundless. A better start, though, is the portrait painted when Milton was ten by

Cornelius Janssen, a young Flemish artist living in London. Janssen's dark background highlights the boy's oval face with its huge, intelligent eyes. The body looks pinched beneath the goldwork of the doublet. When Milton grew up he was to be touchy about his undersized appearance. At Cambridge the college hearties called him 'the Lady of Christ's', and Milton's scornful rejoinders about farm-labourers and beer-swillers sound less than comfortable. In 1652, when he had gone blind, a political opponent, Peter Du Moulin, callously turned to account Virgil's description of Polyphemus, 'A monster, hideous, ugly, huge, bereft of sight', then corrected himself, 'No, not "huge", for nothing is more puny, pale, and shrivelled than he in the whole race of stinging insects'. The bait was knowingly selected. 'My stature, I own, is not tall,' Milton unwisely retorted, 'but may approach nearer to the middle than to the small size.' Anxious assurances follow: he always wore a sword when young, and was 'a match for any man, though far my superior in strength'. Young Milton, from what we hear, put in a lot of fencing practice, and knights in armour, he later recalls, took up a good deal of his reading time. Critics who enjoy fitting poetry to personality might predict that this diminutive swordsman would indulge himself in a hero as sizable as Samson (technicalities in the Samson-Harapha exchange show a continuing interest in duelling).

Why choose Janssen as artist? The answer helps us to get at other roots of Milton's personality. His father was a shrewd businessman, not above turning a dishonest penny. Nominally a 'scrivener' (professional penman) he was essentially a usurer, and made his fortune by arranging loans, handling investments, and buying property. But he also had a passion for music, wrote it himself, and published enough to make his name as a minor composer. His choice of painter speaks for his financial and aesthetic acumen. Janssen later became an expensive court portraitist, but was a nobody in 1618. The elder Milton's acquisitiveness, to be fair, had been needful for survival. He had to fend for himself after his own father, a Catholic with lands at Stanton St. John, near Oxford, disinherited him for his Protestant opinions. Having gone down in the world, he was intent on scrambling up, and, some time before the poet was born, managed to get himself granted a coat of arms—a red eagle on a silver shield—and called his Bread-Street house (the other occupants were a grocer, a girdler, a milliner and a maker of braces) the Spreadeagle.

Thanks to his father Milton did not have to make money with his poetry (*Paradise Lost* went to Symmons, the printer, for £5), or find a job when he left Cambridge. 'Providence', he recalls with satisfaction, 'hath ever bred me up in plenty.' In 1640, back from his cultural tour in Italy (cost: about £400), he agreed to tutor his sister's two boys, and ran a small school in his big new house in Aldersgate. From the few names we know, the pupils were gentlemanly sprigs whose parents could foot the bill, but Milton hardly needed money. He was currently interested in theories of educational reform (see the pamphlet *Of Education*), and wanted guinea-pigs. His Civil-War journalism was not meant to make money either, and did not: 'I supported myself upon my own fortune', he asserts in 1654, grumbling over his tax-returns. He was over forty when he started his only regular job, as secretary for foreign tongues to Cromwell's government (mainly a matter of translating official letters into Latin), at £288 a year. When the Council of State voted him £100 for his *Defence of the English People*, he turned it down, and he died worth £1,500, though he had lost £2,000 at the Restoration. Leisured, moneyed, proudly above selling his pen, Milton was, notwithstanding, almost as ruthless a financier as his father, and was repeatedly involved in litigation. Lending money at interest, he explains in *Christian Doctrine*, is just as decent as any other business venture. His first client, as it happened, was his future father-in-law Richard Powell: the loan, £500. When Powell failed to pay up in 1644, Milton got his hands on the Powell property in Oxfordshire (a painstaking inventory of household goods survives in the poet's hand) and began a series of legal proceedings, pressing his claim doggedly until ten years after Powell's death.

Like any ambitious father, Milton senior impressed on his

13

son the need for effort. 'From the time I was twelve years old,' Milton remembers, 'I scarcely ever went from my lessons to bed before midnight. This, in fact, was the first thing which injured my eyes. They were naturally weak, and I often had headaches.' The boy was sent to St. Paul's unusually early (at seven, probably) and extra tutors were hired to cram his head still tighter at home. Not surprisingly he grew up with a sense of the mediocrity of his fellows. The only intimate friendship he ever seems to have formed was with a younger, gayer boy at St. Paul's, Charles Diodati, whose parents were Italian Protestants living in London. Eventually Charles went to Oxford and Milton to Cambridge, but they could still be together sometimes in the vacations, and exchange letters. Charles shows off by writing his in Greek. He is plainly delighted to be picked out by so fastidious a companion, plans country rambles, 'so that we can enjoy each other's philosophical and learned talk', and pretends to share Milton's sense of isolation. On his side, Milton laid bare his inner life as to no one else:

> I assure you that it is impossible for me not to love such men as yourself, for . . . God has instilled in me a great passion for the beautiful. Ceres never sought her daughter Proserpine with greater ardour than I do this idea of the beautiful, like some image of loveliness, ever pursuing it, by day and by night, in every shape and form . . . And so whenever I find someone who spurns the base opinions of common men . . . I must needs attach myself to that person without delay.
>
> Letter to Diodati, 23 September 1637; Columbia ii, 24–6

A complacent awareness of the level of their conversation colours the enjoyment of both participants.

Among common young men, Milton seems to have felt insecure; scornful of their opinions but avid for their approval. He dreams on the one hand of a scholarly seclusion in which spiritual peace will be won, and on the other of himself festooned with fame and glory while angels and men clap appreciatively. Both dreams are lonely, but in one it is the loneliness of the sage, in the other of the hero. These fantasies provide one of the most insistent tensions in Milton's thought. (Eventually *Paradise Regained* evolved a protagonist who could be a hero and sage at once.) So, while he despised his loutish fellow-students at Cambridge (informing a schoolmaster-friend at St. Paul's that it was not worth conversing with them), he could not resist currying their favour when given a chance. During the summer vacation of 1628 he was chosen to deliver a speech in support of recreation. The result was a compound of dirty jokes and ridicule of the names of college servants—a brand of entertainment for which his talent was very meagre. Similarly, though he thought the educational system at Cambridge a tedious anachronism, no sooner could a senior member breathe his last than Milton was in attendance with a set of piously heartbroken Latin verses. Dr. Gostlin, the Vice-Chancellor, Lancelot Andrewes and Nicholas Felton, both ex-Masters of Pembroke, even Richard Ridding, the beadle, were honoured in this fashion. Young Milton wrote much of the time not because he felt any artistic impulse but because he liked applause. Sending some Greek verses to a friend a couple of years after leaving Cambridge, he admits that he has given up Greek composition: the audience, he explains, is too small. But applause was elusive. Other young men were talked about. There was Thomas Randolph, up at Cambridge with Milton, and already one of the Ben Jonson set in London, with a first volume in print and a fellowship at Trinity besides. Milton, while purloining one or two of Randolph's better bits for his own poems, meditated glumly upon his backwardness—still boyish in looks, and poetically sterile—in the sonnet he wrote on becoming twenty-three. At the end he seems to cheer up: even if 'inward ripeness' has still not arrived:

> Yet be it less or more, or soon or slow,
> > It shall be still in strictest measure ev'n
> > To that same lot, however mean or high,
> Toward which Time leads me, and the will of Heav'n;
> > All is, if I have grace to use it so,
> > As ever in my great task-Master's eye.

SONNET VII, 9–14

A convenient submissiveness, but the meaning is troublesome.

If everything is always in God's eye, then it is so whether Milton has grace to use it so or not. The confident tramp of the closing lines is over thin ice. He enclosed this troubled sonnet in a letter to a former tutor, who had evidently been intimating that he ought to get a job. The letter admits that he wants fame and public employment, and so contrasts strikingly with what he had told his father a couple of years earlier when, leaving Cambridge, he had been allowed to retire to the Buckinghamshire village of Horton, to spend his time bookishly:

> You, father, have not made me go where . . . the golden hope of making money shines bright and clear. . . . Instead you have taken me far away from the din of the city into this deep seclusion, with the intention of enriching my already cultivated mind still further. . . . So I, who already have a place, though a low one, in the ranks of the learned, shall one day sit among those who wear the ivy and laurels of victory. Now I shall no longer mix with the brainless mob: my steps will shun the sight of common eyes.
>
> AD PATREM 68–9, 73–5, 101–4

When Milton entered the arena of pamphlet-controversy at the start of the 1640s, he saw that one of his two dreams had to be relinquished for the time being. The sage 'soaring in the high region of his fancies' had to plunge into 'a troubled sea of noises and hoarse disputes'. But both dreams persisted, and sometimes in the later work they are comically superimposed. In 1655 he tells his ex-pupil Cyriack Skinner that since he lost his sight writing the *Defence of the English People* (a great success: publicly burned in Paris and Toulouse within three months of its publication), he lost it:

> In liberty's defence, my noble task,
> Of which all Europe talks from side to side.
>> This thought might lead me through the world's vain mask
>> Content though blind, had I no better guide.
>
> SONNET XXII, 11–14

The sage, shrugging off the world as a 'vain mask', keeps odd company with the excited pamphleteer who imagines himself the talk of Europe. The *Second Defence* (1654) also accommodates both dreams. The great Fairfax, who had resigned all his commands in 1650 and tucked himself away in Yorkshire to read, and collect coins, is held up as an example: 'You did not subdue the enemy only. You have triumphed too over that flame of ambition and lust of glory which make the best and greatest men their slaves.' But no work lusts for glory more patently: Milton fancies that he is surrounded by the congregated multitudes of Europe, hanging on his words and filling his ears with applause. He needed to believe that his first *Defence* had won him this eminence. How, otherwise, could he bear the thought that political journalism had cost him eyesight and his as yet unwritten epic as well? 'I am far from having spent my efforts, as you seem to hint, on trivial matters,' he replies touchily to a correspondent late in 1654.

The dream of himself as a world-scorning recluse was encouraged by his youthful passion for Platonism. In the neo-Platonic works attributed to the legendary Hermes Trismegistus ('thrice great Hermes' in *Il Penseroso*) he fastened on to the belief that the chaste philosopher could achieve a temporary separation of soul and body, an ecstasy, in which the soul might travel over the earth or up through the spheres of the universe, hearing the music they were supposed to make as they circled, and come into sight of heaven itself. The excitement generated by this idea is apparent in the early poems (see *Vacation Exercise* 33–44, *Il Penseroso* 164–6, *Arcades* 61–73, *Comus* 1018–21), and writing to his father on the threshold of his philosophic retirement to Horton he imagines his spirit already in flight, 'singing, among the starry choirs, a deathless melody, an indescribable song'. The idea was one that reconciled the dreams of hero and sage, because if, through self-discipline and chastity, he could enter these regions of the spirit, he might produce poetry that was divinely inspired—an immortal national epic—and so become a hero, even a saviour, of his nation; for poetry, he believed, was what bred and cherished 'in a great people the seeds of virtue'. And when his epic finally came, Milton held that it was divinely inspired: the fruit of his contact with a spirit-being who visited him at night (in winter only) and dictated verse which he repeated in the morning for whoever was waiting to copy it down. 'Up led by thee,' he writes, 'Into the Heav'n of Heav'ns I have presum'd,/An Earthly Guest, and drawn Empyreal Air' (*PL* vii, 11–15). It is the same flight.

Between the halves of Milton's life sticks out, like a hinge, his stay in Italy. Before it: privacy, Cambridge and Horton. The 1637 edition of *Comus* bears a timid motto from Virgil's *Eclogues*, 'Alas, what was I thinking of, poor wretch, to let the south wind blow on my blossoms . . .' (timid, but edged: Virgil continues '. . . and the boars trample in my clear springs?') After Italy comes the start of his pamphleteering (1641), marriage (1642), and the 1645 collected poems, with a confident motto: 'Crown my brow with leaves and let no hostile tongue do injury to the destined poet.' In Italy he realised what society could be like. He found himself surrounded by witty, well-read young men, who greatly admired his poetry, and their own. In Florence, Rome and Naples he was fêted, argued with, congratulated, taken around and introduced to important people. He went to concerts, heard the glamorous Leonora Baroni sing, and, like everyone else, wrote her adoring verses. He was asked along to meetings of the smart literary academies, with facetious names like 'The Disinclined' and 'The Apathetics', and when he read them his own poems they broke into ecstatic compliments.

> One in whose memory is the whole world; in whose intelligence, wisdom; in whose will, the ardent quest of glory; in whose mouth, eloquence; who, with astronomy as his guide, hears the harmonious sounds of the celestial spheres.
>
> JOANNI MILTONI LONDINIENSI, prefaced to Milton's POEMATA, 1645

No one had talked like that in Bread Street. Milton preserved each garland carefully, and later they turn up as appetisers in the 1645 edition. In Rome, Lukas Holste, one of the librarians, took him round the great Vatican Library, and introduced him to Cardinal Francesco Barberini, the most powerful man in the city, chief councillor to his uncle, Pope Urban, and a splendid patron of scholars and artists. Milton was invited to one of the magnificent Barberini concerts, and the Cardinal himself waited at the door to pick him out from the crush of people. At Naples he was taken to meet Giovanni Battista Manso, Marquis of Villa, who had been Tasso's patron. Flattering verses by Manso himself were added to Milton's collection before he left.

Italy gave Milton a new self-confidence: not fragile arrogance, but the certainty that grows from the praise of strangers freely given. At the same time he lost some of his distrust of society; acquired, even, a taste for gay company which, back in England, he tried unpromisingly to indulge by dropping in, of an evening, on some 'young sparks' of Gray's Inn—'the beaux of those times', they seemed, to his little nephew. The dream of the sage receded. That of the hero took on a firmer outline.

> For whoever in a state knows how to form wisely the character of his people, and to rule them in peace and in war with enlightened laws, him in the first place, above all others, I should esteem worthy of all honour.
>
> Letter to Buonmatheo; 10 September 1638; Columbia xii, 30

he wrote to one of his new Italian friends.

Italy, too, gave a new impetus to Milton's musical interests. At home with his father he had learnt the organ and the bass-viol (a sort of 'cello), and now he shipped home 'a chest or two of choice music books' which included works by Monteverdi, Marenzio, Vecchi, Gesualdo and Cifra. What these are all engaged in is the fusing of words and music, a problem Milton and the composer Henry Lawes had already tackled in *Comus*. Monteverdi is the revolutionary: the first composer to make the poetic word regulate and determine the harmony (as Milton said it should in his sonnet to Lawes). He was in charge of the St. Mark's choir in Venice while Milton was there. The city had two opera houses, and he may have seen something of the composer's performed. In Florence Milton became a member of the same literary group as Giovanni Battista Doni, who was gripped by the current Italian enthusiasm for musical drama, and who turned Seneca's *Troades* into an opera, arguing for a technique based largely on recitative, which would highlight the significance of the words. Milton, when he got home, started writing *Paradise Lost* as a drama (*Adam Unparadised*) and it looks as if this may have been a cross between opera and Greek play, with angelic choruses, and the story told in recitative (at this stage he wrote Satan's address to the sun, iv, 30–41). Eventually he let Dryden turn *Paradise Lost* into an opera.

Milton's interest in Italian harmonic experimentation is matched by this enthusiasm for the *avant-garde* versification of Della Casa and Tasso, which he had studied before he went to Italy (his copy of Della Casa has the purchase-date 1629). Della Casa gave his sonnets a complicated word-order by devices like inversion and interpolation, to create the impression of a syntax near to that of Latin. By multiplying pauses within the lines and manipulating clauses to chop across the line- and quatrain-divisions he made his verse sound toughly meaningful. Milton's sonnets follow suit, but a sonnet is a limiting form, and his ear was eager for the more complex sound-effects that an elongated, irregular stanza could produce. Hence his cultivation of the Italian *canzone* (the stanza-form of *Upon the Circumcision* copies Petrarch's *canzone* to the Virgin), and of the loosened-up *canzone*, developed by Tasso and others, which gives almost boundless opportunities for richness and innovation of aural pattern. This is how the verse-form of *Lycidas* evolved. *On Time* and *At a Solemn Music* are experiments on the way. More challenging still was the idea of writing a whole epic in which the verbal texture of each paragraph would be as dense as that of a Della Casa sonnet, and the musical subtleties as diversified as those of the *canzone*. This concept, another growth-point for *Paradise Lost*, came to Milton via Tasso who had adapted Della Casa's innovations to epic use in his masterpiece, *Jerusalem Delivered* (1581). Giving up rhyme for blank verse, to make the rhythmic unit more adaptable, was another step Tasso had taken, in his 8,000-line poem on the creation of the world. When he got back from Italy Milton felt that his epic was going to be like nothing there had been in English before—'new and lofty measures'—intricate, difficult. It had to wait fifteen years. He tried his hand at it, though, as soon as he got home, but found he could not keep it up—he tells his Italian friends about this in a poem on Diodati's death which he sent them in 1640.

But even if Milton's metrics can be made to look advanced, what, it may be asked, can be done about his attitude towards women? He did, of course, think them usually (not always) less intelligent than men: everyone in his century thought so. But the most determined critic could not make him look like a misogynist. He married three times, and the most moving of his poems mourns the death of his second wife. He enjoyed the company of educated, elegant women like Lady Margaret Ley and Mrs. Catharine Thomason—both remembered in sonnets— and the brilliant young Viscountess Ranelagh. When he was twenty he fell in love with an Italian girl living in London, which is what his sonnet to the nightingale and his Italian poems are about (in one of them he hid her name, Emilia). As a young man his favourite reading was the delicately lascivious adventures of Ovid and Tibullus. One, in which Ovid describes what ensued when Corinna came stealing almost naked to his bedroom one blazing noonday, stuck in his mind fixedly enough for a line of it to turn up at the end of his funeral poem for the Bishop of Winchester. His copy of William Browne's *Britannia's Pastorals* (1613–16) is appreciatively annotated with comments like 'A beautiful maid' and 'A beautiful virgin undressing herself', to recall his attention to passages of interest. We find him confiding to Diodati how at eighteen he used to lurk in an elm-grove in the London suburbs to spy on the parties of young girls who passed by, and how excited their light-blown hair and the flush of their complexions made him. Later he writes about how he fell in love with one of these beautiful creatures, but while he was plucking up courage to follow her, she disappeared in the crowd. It may not really have happened, of course: the image of a perfect woman, glimpsed, then snatched away, fascinated him. It provides the climax of the sonnet on his dead wife, and in *Paradise Lost* ix, 385–411, Eve slips her hand from Adam's and disappears among the trees, never to be seen perfect again. If your ideal woman is pure and elusive, the real thing may come as a surprise. Milton, who married suddenly and confidently in

1642 (Mary Powell, the daughter of an Oxfordshire squire, and only seventeen—half his age—was the bride), took time to adjust. Meanwhile Mary went home. Her family, who owed him money, had probably pushed her into marrying him ('what more usual,' he wrote later, 'than the persuasion of friends that acquaintance, as it increases, will amend all?'). Milton began another affair with the 'handsome and witty' daughter of a Dr. Davis and wrote some wearisome treatises arguing (indisputably enough) that divorce should be legal in cases of intellectual incompatibility as well as adultery. Good citizens brayed in protest. Eventually Mary came back and within a year a child was born, but the language of the divorce tracts (Milton talks about being bound fast 'to an image of earth and phlegm' and condemned to 'grind in the mill of an undelighted and servile copulation') remains to show what a shock he had. Later heroes —Adam and Samson—reflect his susceptibility to women. Even Christ (*PR* ii, 353–61) is tempted by girls in a distant grove like those who promenaded unknowingly past Milton. In the poem written to his father at the start of his monastic retreat to Horton, Milton imagines Knowledge as a naked girl bending her face down for him to kiss.

We are on safer ground in suspecting that Milton was humourless: the only great English poet, apart from Wordsworth, to be so. The few jokes which survive—those of God and Satan in *Paradise Lost*, for instance—are in cruel taste. So is the Greek epigram Milton got William Marshall to inscribe under a portrait he had engraved for the collected poems of 1645. Milton, always vain about his looks, thought the likeness unflattering, and the words Greekless Marshall copied invited onlookers to 'laugh at a rotten picture by a good-for-nothing artist'. 'He pronounced the letter "R" very hard—a certain sign of satirical wit,' Dryden told Aubrey, the 17th-century gossip-gatherer. What disconcerts about this type of humourlessness in a great imaginative artist is that it is so unimaginative, so tightly self-regarding.

Another stumbling-block, Milton's erudition, can be by-passed more easily. He was learned, of course, but the bewildered assumption that he had read everything, which annotated editions encourage, may be discarded. Like any Renaissance man of letters, he referred to a good many authors whom he knew only in scraps, from dictionaries, grammars or rhetorics. Besides, the erudition intrudes more in the prose than the poetry. An appreciative reading of modern translations of the *Iliad*, *Odyssey*, *Aeneid* and Ovid's *Metamorphoses* will allow even the unclassical to respond to the great majority of Milton's poetic allusions (and this is much less than you need for Eliot or Pound). His reading seems less daunting, too, if the English poets he enjoyed are looked at. He soon realised that Shakespeare and Spenser (a favourite of his schoolmaster, Alexander Gill) were enviably talented, and requisitioned their phrases liberally, but he was impressed, too, by trumpery like Joshua Sylvester's translation (1605) of the French poet Du Bartas's biblical epic on the creation and history of mankind. Better, though hardly a masterpiece, was William Browne's *Britannia's Pastorals* which let the young Milton into an England (its charms on loan from Spenser and Ovid) of dewy flowers, bird-song and running water, with shepherds playing harmlessly at sex and fairies dancing under the moon. Much the same ingredients went into Fletcher's pastoral play *The Faithful Shepherdess* which gave Milton the idea for *Comus*. Outside literature his attitude towards knowledge was firmly utilitarian. He had no patience with grammarians or philologists and insisted that schoolboys should be moved on to reading authors as quickly as possible, and pick up the grammar as they went along. At Cambridge, the endless intricacies of scholastic logic left him 'half dead with boredom'. The exasperation is attractive, but has its perils. Distrust of subtle argument will find itself cutting knots irritably when it takes on issues like the fall of man and God's foreknowledge. Our qualms about the rough justice in *Paradise Lost* might be eased by some patient logical unravelling of a kind on which, in the poem, only the devils fritter away their time (ii, 555–61).

The same fierce simplicity can be seen in his religious beliefs. He worked these out, from the text of the Bible, in a book called *Christian Doctrine* which was lost for over a century and is so unorthodox that when it turned up in 1823 many Christians refused to believe him the author. In it he rejects the doctrine of the Trinity—'all that play-acting of the persons of the godhead'—maintaining with dogged common sense that if Christ is a Son he cannot be the same age as his father. Since Adam and Eve's souls, not their bodies, sinned, he argues, their souls not their bodies must have been punished with death. Therefore the human soul dies with the body, and stays in the grave till the end of the world. The solution to another theological riddle, 'What did God make the world out of?' (orthodox answer: 'Nothing'), seemed to him, as usual, obvious: only God is eternal, so before he made the world there was only him, so he made it out of himself. These three heresies (subordinationism, mortalism, materialism) were not new, but Milton warns his readers not to write him off as an imitator: it is the spirit of free enquiry, he says, that has determined his conclusions. Predictably *Christian Doctrine* is unconventional about marriage, as well. Marriage is merely a civil matter: its celebration not the function of a minister of religion. Abraham and Moses had more than one wife, and God made David a present of several. Therefore polygamy is a legal form of marriage. A wife should be able to leave her husband if she has been badly treated, and a man should be able to send any of his wives packing if they prove quarrelsome (Abraham, again, set a useful example with Hagar). Milton's 'Hail wedded love' means 'Hail polygamy and easy divorce'.

Milton ends up looking so far from Puritanical as to be hardly, to most people's way of thinking, a recognisable Christian at all. At the Restoration his enemies were able to ridicule him as an irrepressible free-thinker: 'an old heretic both in religion and manners, that by his will would shake off his governors as he doth his wives, four in a fortnight. . . . He is so much an enemy to usual practices that I believe when he is condemned to travel to Tyburn in a cart, he will petition for the favour to be the first man that ever was driven thither in a wheelbarrow.' The popular image of black-suited narrowness which we began with has to be supplemented with something more adventurous before it

24

will be any use. We need to keep in mind as we read the poems the emancipated author who (in *Areopagitica*) stood out against the suppression of books, the revolutionary whose imagination was seized by the thought of beheading a king, and the artist who pursued his idea of the beautiful 'by day and by night, in every shape and form'.

# 2

# Leaving the Earth: The *Nativity Ode*

Just after Christmas 1629 Milton sent Charles Diodati a Latin verse-letter (Elegy 6) announcing that he had written the *Nativity Ode*. It came to him, Milton says, as an inspiration, at dawn on Christmas Day. Partly, though, he was remembering an Italian poem he had read recently. Tasso's *On the Day of the Nativity*, like Milton's *Ode*, contrasts the courts of everlasting day and their harmony with the dark house Christ comes to, and mentions Nature's awe, the world-wide peace, Apollo and the dumb oracles, Lybic Hammon, Osiris's 'lowings' and the barking Anubis. Tasso ends his *canzone* by offering his 'humble' poem and comparing it with the 'odours sweet' that the magi bring.

What made Tasso's poem germinate in Milton's mind? A diminutive Christ routing huge beast-gods possibly had satisfying aspects for Milton who, sword at side, reckoned himself 'a match for any man, though far my superior in strength'. Both, too, were starting their careers: Milton had just celebrated his twenty-first birthday. The verse-letter to Diodati includes some self-dedication. From now on he will live like an epic poet. Vegetarianism and chastity are to be enforced. We shall consider later the effect that this restrictive temper had on the *Ode*.

From Tasso's assortment of traditional Christmas properties, Milton took the pagan gods and made their expulsion his poem's climax. Why? It is clear that Milton was deeply responsive to pagan myth. It had power and warmth and two great literatures to recommend it. The figures he found in Ovid, Virgil and Homer had for years inhabited his imagination more vividly than the real people he met at St. Paul's or Christ's. The peopled landscape in which sun and dawn evolved into richly-storied presences, Phoebus and Aurora, appealed poignantly. But it could not be defended against the truths of Christianity. A tension ensued which fractures Milton's early poems, and survives in the retractions tied to the tails of great mythological creations in *Paradise Lost* (e.g. i, 746–7).

Milton's richest reconstruction of the pagan vista was the fifth Latin elegy. Written a few months before the *Ode*, it imagines the springtime earth as a girl, bent on seducing the sun. Her figure is attentively rounded out: dewy hair; flowers twined in it; rosy breath; breasts provocatively uncovered. She murmurs reproaches when the sun ungallantly subsides into the sea. Meanwhile other creatures follow earth's example. The wood-gods, Pan, Sylvanus (half-goat, half-god) and satyrs scurry through flower-covered meadows at the heels of none-too-reluctant nymphs. Each grove has its local deity. Milton prays that the gods may never leave their homes among the trees, and that the golden age may return to 'this wretched world': the time of which the Roman poets had sung, before the coming of sin, when man lived instinctively and wandered the earth in delight. The *Nativity Ode* also craves for this age of innocence (133–5), but chases off the brutish gods and the nymphs which the fifth elegy had invited to stay.

The *Ode* begins to look like a piece of mind-cleansing. True, the classical gods do not get the worst of it, though Apollo (176) features among the refugees. But Milton knew by now that the Syrian and Egyptian deities, who bear the brunt of the poem's attack, were not really to be distinguished from the darlings of his classical imagination. By the time he wrote the *Ode* his interest in comparative religion had taken him to John Selden's modernistic *Assyrian Gods* (a new edition came out in 1629). There he read theories which connected the ghastly details of Moloch worship (205–10)—the furnace, the children tipped into it, the priests clashing cymbals to drown the screams—with the Roman Saturn, ruler of the golden age. He found the Syrian Thammuz (204) and the Egyptian Osiris (213) identified with Adonis, and the Syrian Ashtaroth (200) with Venus. Some of this he had known or guessed already, from classical writers, but seeing it

worked out in this 17th-century *Golden Bough* can hardly have
made him feel more comfortable about his affection for paganism.

The *Ode* amputates the pagan half of his poetic life. The
surgeon sounds reluctant:

> The lonely mountains o'er,
> And the resounding shore,
>     A voice of weeping heard, and loud lament;
> From haunted spring and dale
> Edg'd with poplar pale,
>     The parting Genius is with sighing sent,
> With flow'r-inwov'n tresses torn
> The Nymphs in twilight shade of tangled thickets mourn.

181–8

Difficult, after this, to realise we are not meant to pity these
desolate Ophelias. Especially difficult, since even Milton finds
himself remembering the slaughter of the innocents in *Matthew*
ii, 18: 'In Rama was there a voice heard, lamentation and weeping and great mourning, Rachel weeping for her children, and
would not be comforted.' To innocents and nymphs, Christ's
birth brought disaster. And though the pagan gods leave by
one door, they return by others. Nature, anyway, still thinks
of the moon as 'Cynthia's seat' (103), even after she has seen her
'great Master', and Christ is called 'the mighty Pan' (89), and
implicitly likened to the infant Hercules strangling a snake in his
cradle (226–8). The Renaissance had likened him to Pan and to
Hercules before, of course, but the effect of replacing pagan
figures into a poem which rejects paganism can scarcely be got
over by citing precedents. The temper is modified. If Pan and
Hercules and Cynthia, however disinfected, can be rescued, the
rout of pagan values stops short of finality. A look at the poem's
middle section suggests other elements which counter its Jack-
the-Giantkiller Christianity. Even Moloch's blue flames (205–9)
seem innocuous compared with the Old Testament God's world-
shattering fireworks six stanzas earlier (156–64); and the swords
and helmets of God's angels (112–13) look suspicious in the
general disarmament (55).

The second direction which the *Ode* takes, it maintains more

28

undividedly. It is resolutely less human and natural than Milton's readers might have expected.

To explain this we must return to Elegy 6 where Milton distinguishes sharply between the way of life of the epic poet and of the poet who wrote love-elegies. The elegiac poet was expected to depict his own affairs, or pretend to. Ovid's elegies, and those of imitators like Donne, depend upon human drama and authenticity, in a realistic urban setting. A girl catches Ovid's eye, he follows her to the chariot races, gets a seat next to hers, and edges up against her. She tries to wriggle away but the crush is too great. He notices the hem of her skirt in the dust, and stoops to pick it up, apparently helpful but actually trying to get a look at her legs. What he sees makes him still more determined. All the while the poem keeps up a suggestive commentary on events in the arena—the starting-gates flying open, the drivers hugging the bends or creeping up on the inside. Milton's Elegy 7 about the girl he glimpsed in a crowd, though more romantic, aims to sound equally matter-of-fact. Milton felt obliged to disown it and the other elegies in his collected poems of 1645, adding some lines about the 'warped mind and base spirit' that had been responsible. In Elegy 6 he leaves love-poetry to the more sociable Diodati, advising him to cultivate the company of girls. To show the kind of thing Diodati will find useful, Milton describes a dance in the tapestried gallery of a 17th-century country house—perfume, music, bright eyes—the scene effervesces into a stream of excited sensory responses, their range and detail suggesting complete involvement on Milton's part. But all this he is renouncing. By contrast he assigns to himself in the elegy a rusty handful of epic currency: Jove, Cerberus, wars. His determination to turn himself into an epic poet reads like self-emasculation.

One other thing Elegy 6 contains is a preview of the *Nativity Ode* in the form of a list of topics treated in the poem. Warned by the elegy's frosty subjection of the natural man, we might have guessed that the one element in the preview left out of the final version would be the most human: 'the infant cries of God'. Milton's 'dreaded Infant' is dry-eyed. Other naturalistic aspects were rejected even before the preview. Mary's motherhood must have been tucked out of sight early on. Milton's 'wedded Maid, and Virgin Mother' (3), with all the bloodlessness of paradox, stays on the poem's furthest edge. She may be wedded, but her husband does not appear. The other mother in the *Ode* is lonely and deserted too—Ashtaroth, 'Heav'n's Queen and Mother both' (201). The titles suggest Mary, and Ashtaroth's fate becomes a Puritan caveat against Virgin-worship. Readers accustomed to seeing her watch over her sleeping child sometimes fail to notice how she is finally hustled away from Christ. 'See the Virgin blest' (237): but the figure who is seen, five lines later, 'Her sleeping Lord with Handmaid Lamp attending' (242), turns out, on inspection, to be a star. Richard Crashaw, writing within twenty years of Milton, brings the shepherds indoors (in Milton they stay on the grass) to watch an altogether warmer scene:

> The babe no sooner 'gan to seek
>   Where to lay his lovely head,
> But straight his eye advised his cheek
> 'Twixt mother's breasts to go to bed.
> 'Sweet choice', said I, 'no way but so,
> Not to lie cold, yet sleep in snow.'

A HYMN OF THE NATIVITY 47–52

It is not that Crashaw is more cuddlesome. The doctrine of the incarnation cannot be expressed unless the artist can manage a flesh-and-blood baby. Preserving the 'dreaded Infant's' dignity will deprive him of point. Painters and poets in the Renaissance enlivened Christ and his mother with naturalistic accessories, putting the fleshliness of incarnation into the child's sprawling nakedness and the full breasts of the madonna. Milton shrinks from this. His Christ is not seen until safely 'wrapped' (31, 228), and has bed-clothes, it is suggested, pulled primly to his chin (229–31). The 'Sun-in-bed' image deftly removes the manger, and substitutes a four-poster with red curtains. The fact that Christ was even born naked is conceded only partially: Nature, to 'sympathise' with him, 'Had doff't her gawdy trim' (33–4), but that might mean that Nature, and Christ, retained a modest minimum. And in the next stanza, where Nature begs for a white veil to cover her 'naked shame', the reader is advised to look for nakedness only from the neck up. It is her 'front' (i.e. forehead or face) that needs covering. Milton's provision of skirts for his fays (235)—the only detail attached to them—betrays a similar awkwardness about flesh. Even the night is 'shame-fac't' (111) until it has been 'array'd' (dressed).

Sexually the Nature of the *Ode* is sadly shrunken. In Elegy 5 she was lavishly abandoned. Now her fruitful play ends (35–6). Human love becomes something which might, at best, occupy the 'silly thoughts' of shepherds (91). 'Silly' already bore its modern meaning when Milton wrote, though susceptible of less offensive ones like 'pitiable' or 'simple'. 'Silly sheep' was a poetic cliché from Spenser's *Shepherd's Calendar*. Milton, shifting the adjective from sheep to masters, gave it keener edge. The *Ode* celebrates not love but restraint. Christ triumphs in 'control' (228). He binds the vigorous dragon (169). The only kiss in the poem is between wind and sea (65).

However loudly the angels sing, however brightly they shine, they do not disguise the neutered coldness which spreads from the poem's opening. The fiery coal (28) with which Milton imagines his lips being touched, is placed by the next line in a huge landscape of 'winter wild'. Snow gleams through the next stanza (39–42)—(Milton self-consciously avoids putting snow in the Middle East by making Christ, a stanza later, send down Peace instead (46), but the reader retains the impression that snow has fallen). The halcyons hatching their eggs on the sea (68), and the shepherds sitting on the grass in the small hours (86–7), substitute raw exposure for the warm associations of nest and pastoral. Cold starlight persists unnaturally (69–72). The sun is prevented from bringing his 'burning Axletree' to melt the scene. (Milton took the phrase from a contrast between the sun's heat and intense cold in Chapman's *Bussy d'Ambois*: 'fly where men feel/The burning axletree, and those that suffer/Beneath the chariot of the snowy Bear'.) The 'new-enlight'n'd' world, deprived of the sun's 'flame' (81–2), shows itself in a chill glitter upon metallic 'helmed' and 'sworded' figures (112–13).

The figure, it is worth noticing, who tries to get the life-giving power of the sun back, and drive the stars away, is Lucifer (74). The name could mean the morning star (Venus) or the sun or the devil (following *Isaiah* xiv, 12). The first fits the context, as representative of fleshly love, but the choice of name designedly connects the figure with the sun and Satan as well. Christ's tussle with the 'old Dragon' has begun already. The 'squadrons' of heaven's 'spangled host' stay where they are, waiting his word of command (a third of their number fall in *Paradise Lost* through listening to Satan's). But Satan is on the side of nature.

Probably the ox and the ass are the bits of naturalness most people are sorriest to lose. They have every right to be there. Spenser's nativity scene had told how Christ: 'encradled was/ In simple cratch, wrapped in a wad of hay,/Between the toilful ox and humble ass.' Milton leaves the animals out, and flaunts his omission. Osiris 'Trampling the unshow'r'd Grass with lowings loud' (215) can hardly help drawing attention to the gap. Nor can the 'Bright-harness'd' angels (244). Of course 'harnessed' means 'wearing armour', as it often did in the 17th century. But the word's other meaning impudently draws attention to what is not there.

Milton's Christ, then, is emphatically not a helpless, naked baby, hanging at his mother's breasts, breathed on by cattle, laid in straw, gaped at by yokels. He is a prince, cold, dignified, immensely strong, already the terror of his enemies, lying in a curtained bed with an astral attendant and an armed guard. The poem does not drift away from our affections, it is steered. The direction is that of Elegy 6.

In the *Ode*'s structure the effort towards a clear-cut design, and the insistence upon control are unmistakable. The poem takes the form of a triptych. In the first of its three leaves, quiet is almost unbroken. Only the subdued chatter of shepherds is heard, as of a waiting audience. Lighting is gradually stepped up. In the course of the sixth stanza 'glimmering' stars in a brightening sky before sunrise (73–9) take over from their more decidedly nocturnal 'steadfast gaze' (70). Immobility grips every creature. 'Kings sat still with awful eye' (59) gives the eye itself a stoniness. In this ominous stillness Christ's control is shown by his despatch of Peace (45) and peremptory command to the stars (76).

In the second leaf of the triptych (93–172) reverberating ('thrilling') sound and supernatural light break out. The sound develops from the 'noise' (95) of heaven's orchestral concert, to the 'chime' (128) of the spheres, and the 'clang' (157) on Sinai; the light, from 'glittering' (114) angels, to 'Celestial sheen' (145), to 'red fire' (159). At the same time the poem springs into movement with the arrival of the animated cherubim and seraphim, the revolving spheres and exploding mountain. The examples of control grow gigantic with the hanging of the world 'on hinges' (122), the pushing of the elements into place (124), and, at the end of the section, the imprisonment of the 'bound' and 'folded' dragon (168–72) (the participles suggest vigour cramped and trussed). The rigid time-scheme of salvation gets thunderously reasserted, in reply to two rash attempts to speed it up. First Nature, hearing the angelic music, 'almost' believes that the end of the world has come, and that the harmony between heaven and earth that existed before the fall has been restored (101–8). Then Milton, leaping from the Bethlehem scene back into 1629, wishes that the end would come (125–32), the golden age return, the sphere-music be heard on earth again, as the neo-Platonists supposed it was before the fall, and the earth ('the Bass of Heav'n's deep Organ') once more add its note to those of the planets. 'But wisest Fate says no' (149). God clamps down on wishful thinking. The plan must grind to its horrible climax.

> The Babe lies yet in smiling Infancy,
> That on the bitter cross
> Must redeem our loss.

151–3

By locating 'Babe', 'smiling' and 'cross' in consecutive lines Milton transforms the act of redemption from an adult sacrifice to the impaling of an unsuspecting baby. Nothing so savage is laid to the account of the heathen gods. The poem's cruellest moment drives home the iron will of 'wisest Fate'. For all the lip-service to 'Trinal Unity' (11), the verb 'Must' implies that Milton already imagines a Son subordinated to the Father's all-powerful control, as in *Christian Doctrine* and *Paradise Lost*.

The roar, the glare and the harshness die away in the third leaf of the triptych to rumblings and fading squeals (173–8) and the quiet sobbing of the victims (183). The cymbals at the 'dismal' dance, and the hollow lowings of Osiris (210, 215) are the loudest sounds. 'Nightly' (179), 'shade' (188) and 'midnight' (191) sweep darkness back across the poem. The last flash of supernatural light blinds a lowing animal, like the one that might have watched over the manger (223).

The shape of Milton's stanza (a6 a6 b10 c6 c6 b10 d8 d12) was his own invention, though the example of Italian verse-forms helped him to evolve it. Stanza, like structure, breaks into three sections: two of three lines, linked by rhyme and line-length, then two lines separated by both, and dragging a final alexandrine to echo the long withdrawal of the pagan gods.

An element that draws attention to the lack of humanity is Milton's animated landscape. Theoretically discrediting the pagan countryside-gods, he consoles himself by alluding to natural events as if they were human. Nature and the sun are personified; the 'gentle Air' can be wooed (38); winds kiss and whisper to the sea (64–6); stars gaze (70). Peace (46) belongs to another troop of make-believes that help to steal the action of the poem from the Holy Family. Equipped with olive-crown, wings and wand she appears as an actor in a masque. So do Truth, Justice and Mercy (141–4) and the 'youngest-teemed Star' in her 'polished Car' (240–1). A masque-like sensationalism is inherent in the *Ode*'s planning: hush, followed by explosion, followed by reverberations. The poet is evidently impressed by the spectacular (glittery angels, for instance), and keeps noticing the spectators' eyes: Christ's eyes watching Nature (43), the 'meek' eyes of Peace (46), the 'awful eye' of the Kings (59), the 'gaze' of the stars (70), the 'pale-ey'd' priest (180), the 'dusky' eyes of Osiris (213). The centre of the poem is imagined in terms of performance: orchestra, choir, organ (128–30). This theatricality stiffens the action, and the writing, at times. The angels solemnly 'harping' with swords and helmets on are clumsily visualised. Truth and Justice wearing 'Th' enamel'd Arras of the Rainbow' (143) have obviously got it from a theatre wardrobe. Mercy is 'With radiant feet the tissued clouds down steering' (146), but we are not meant to ask how she manages to steer clouds with her feet. She is really sitting on clouds made of buckram, or some such stuff ('tissued' meant 'embroidered with gold or silver thread') and would have to be lowered by stage machinery.

Though the *Ode* records how God came down to earth, it points itself in the opposite direction. Milton's dream of seclusion and escape lies behind its most intensely-stated requirements: release into a new golden age, ringing with sphere-music (125–48). Correspondingly, human activity is cut out of the poem and movement supplied by the behaviour of theatrical figures.

# 3

## How the other half lives: *L'Allegro* and *Il Penseroso*

No one knows when *L'Allegro* (The Cheerful Man) or *Il Penseroso* (The Pensive Man) were written. Scholars have shuttled them between 1629 and 1634, or beyond. Some claim to spot features of the Cambridge, some of the Horton countryside, but, rightly, neither side is convinced. There has also been discontent about how the poems relate to each other. Dr. Johnson thought them too alike: no mirth in the melancholy, but some melancholy in the mirth. Later critics have catalogued the similarities. On the subject of melancholy the two poems are found actually to be in agreement. The kind of melancholy chased out of *L'Allegro* is not that welcomed into *Il Penseroso*. The 17th century inherited two theories about what too much melancholy (black bile) did to you. According to Greek medicine it brought reasonless sorrow and illusions—the 'horrid shapes, and shrieks, and sights unholy' of *L'Allegro*'s melancholy. According to Aristotle it made you a philosopher and a poet. Renaissance neo-Platonists extended this idea, celebrating melancholy as the contemplative temper which allowed the soul to leave the body, bound for spiritual heights—*Il Penseroso*'s melancholy.

It has been claimed, too, that the attention paid to light- and sound-effects makes the poems more alike than they seem. *Il Penseroso*'s 'civil-suited' morn breaks under a covering (kerchief) of cloud (122–5); *L'Allegro*'s, also, 'Rob'd', and clouded (60–2). Though at first glance *L'Allegro* is the more brightly-lit poem, its 'Sunshine Holiday' (98) turns out to consist of dancing in the 'Checker'd shade' (96) and stories told when daylight has failed

(99), implying an *Il Penseroso*-like distaste for bright light. Similarly the clear distinction between the first poem's noisiness and the second's quiet (startling lark-song and 'lively din' of cockerel, as against noise-shunning nightingale and bellman's 'drowsy charm') is upset when Il Penseroso opts for 'pealing Organ' and 'full-voic'd Choir' (161–2), while L'Allegro exits to 'soft' airs (136).

When all the links have been unearthed, though, the poems remain opposed. The most that can be said is that they offer not two different personalities, but two ways of life open to the same reticent, rather sad figure. L'Allegro seems more aware than Il Penseroso of the 'sorrow' (45) and 'eating cares' (135) that underlie joy. His 'Then to the Spicy Nut-brown Ale' (100) has the true note of simulated enthusiasm. He is supposed not to shun his fellow men (walking 'not unseen', 57; Il Penseroso, 'unseen', 65). But Mirth, Jest, Jollity, Laughter, and the other sociable abstractions he invokes (11–32), have nothing to do with the life he leads, and he seems at pains to avoid much contact with people. Ploughman, milkmaid, mower and shepherd, whistle, sing, whet a scythe and chatter (63–8), and L'Allegro hears them. But they are removed by a full-stop from the landscape-pleasures which he explicitly looks at (69). He sees the castle, not the girl (77–80); the cottage, not the rustics inside (81–4). City-dwellers are merely a 'busy hum' (118). He substitutes story-book figures ('Knights and barons') for real people. The English peasantry disappear behind classical masks—Corydon, Thyrsis, Phillis. His poem drifts further and further from actual life, through 'masque' and 'pageantry' into dream (128–30).

The question whether L'Allegro ever gets round to speaking to another person is raised, then shelved. 'Then to come ... And at my window bid good-morrow' (45–6)—but who to? If there is anyone outside the window, the reader is not allowed a look. The allusion to Jonsonian comedy a bit later (132) may mean that Milton was remembering Volpone's first line, 'Good morning to the day' (*Volpone* was revived in the 1620s with Burbage in the title-part), and that L'Allegro has no one to talk to.

Still, L'Allegro's seclusion is relative: Il Penseroso's absolute.

In the course of his day he does not even see a living creature. *L'Allegro*'s stage-players dwindle in the second poem to a page of Greek read in solitude (96–100). Nightingale (56), bellman (83) and bee (142–3) exist only as sounds. The choir, a sound too (164), releases the eye from earthly sights altogether. Even the sheep have vanished. L'Allegro noticed them nibbling (72). Il Penseroso finds the close-cropped grass where they have been (66).

L'Allegro has lively enough instincts. Innocent-looking 'Towers and Battlements' (77) start him thinking about women. Smiles that 'love to live in dimple sleek' (30) (the trailing adjective beautifully smoothing the dimple away), Phillis's 'neat' hands (85) and the 'bright eyes' of town ladies (121) engage his imagination. He recommends marriage—for other people, anyway (125). Il Penseroso cautiously places sex out of reach. His heroine, a nun (31), must cover her shoulders and make herself 'decent' (36). He quickly qualifies his invitation, 'Come', with instructions that she should keep her eyes to herself (39–44): she must look either at the sky or the ground. The precautions are curiously specific: Il Penseroso does not want to take any risks with his lovely negress.

L'Allegro feasts (127); Il Penseroso fasts (46). The choice Milton explained to Diodati in Elegy 6 between the epic-orientated recluse and the love-poet, painting from life, is rephrased in the twin poems. Hence the allocation of 'low' literary forms—comedy and pastoral—to *L'Allegro*, and 'high' tragedy and Spenserian epic (116–20) to *Il Penseroso*. The word 'contend' (124) places L'Allegro in a competitive world; whereas Il Penseroso cultivates his garden (50). So behind the poems hover, too, Milton's dreams: the hero at 'high triumphs' (120) in the first, the sage (168–9) in the second.

Following the line taken in Elegy 6, *Il Penseroso* comes out on top. The conduct of the two Orpheus-figures is a pointer. *L'Allegro*'s reclines to 'Lydian airs' that would have won Pluto 'to have quite set free' Eurydice (149–50). Of the ancient modes, the Lydian was held the most effeminate—condemned by Plato as morally enervating. Here it corrupts justice. *Il Penseroso*'s

Orpheus, on the other hand, resembles Christ, who also 'made Hell grant what Love did seek' (108)—the Renaissance was quite used to seeing Orpheus as a version of the Good Shepherd.

The syntax of *L'Allegro*, too, suggests a poet unwilling to be mixed up in his speaker's activities. The pronoun 'I' appears only once, in a guardedly conditional clause (37): elsewhere the poem avoids first-person constructions, though *Il Penseroso* is full of them. Instead *L'Allegro*'s actions are distributed among participles —'listening' (53), 'walking' (57)—and infinitives—'To live' (39), 'To hear' (41)—only hazily connected with any specific agent. The poem twice resorts to a construction—'Then to the Spicy Nut-brown Ale' (100) and 'Then to the well-trod stage' (131)— which sounds unanimous without committing itself to a grammatical subject at all. Verbs are left indefinitely objectless (who do the hamlets (92) 'invite'?), and the plural 'us' (117) also releases the poet from particular involvement. Compared with *Il Penseroso*, *L'Allegro* is a faceless poem. The endings also tip the balance in *Il Penseroso*'s favour: 'if thou canst give' (151) dilutes the address to Mirth with doubt, as against the sturdy 'These pleasures Melancholy give' (175).

Milton shifts confidence from *L'Allegro* into *Il Penseroso* because he is set on release from the earth and the second poem demonstrates how to achieve ecstasy; the first, how not to. Melancholy herself enters on the brink of ecstasy, her soul 'rapt', her chief attendant, Contemplation (54), indicating by his soaring and throne-guiding that he has come from *Ezekiel* ix and x, and is the cherub who lifted the prophet to his vision of God's throne, and tried to keep Milton airborne in *The Passion* (36–8). Music elevates Il Penseroso himself to 'ecstasies' and a sight of heaven (165–6). By contrast, *L'Allegro*'s music can release, Milton says, only the 'soul of harmony' (144), not man's soul. It is difficult to see what releasing the soul of harmony can mean: Milton seems to have forced this secular parody of ecstasy into *L'Allegro* at the expense of some fuzziness.

The heaven that fasting and chastity may raise Il Penseroso to is not represented as purely Christian. The Muses, singing round Jove's altar (47–8), seem strangers in the world of nuns and stained glass (159), and adumbrate the conflict of the *Nativity Ode*. This reminds us that the spirit's flight from earth and the renunciation of soul-clogging sex were prominent elements in the pagan gnosticism which Milton found in the writings attributed to 'thrice great Hermes' (88); so was the pursuit of universal knowledge (*gnosis*) embracing 'every Star' and 'every Herb' (171-2), and including knowledge of those 'Daemons' (93) who ruled the elements and whose names had to be mastered before the gnostic initiate could wing his way upwards. A far cry from 'Hail wedded love' and from Raphael's cautions about knowing 'at large of things remote/From use' (*PL* viii, 191-2). Further, Il Penseroso, unlike his counterpart, still cherishes in his countryside the soft presences of paganism. The secular man's day contains natural happenings: the 'lark' flies (41), the 'dawn' rises (44). Il Penseroso, though, hears not the nightingale, but 'Philomel' (56); sees not the dawn, but 'civil-suited Morn', Aurora, who hunted with Cephalus, 'the Attic Boy' (122-4); not the moon, but 'Cynthia' (59). He searches among the trees for Silvanus, the the Roman wood-god (134), and the nymphs, not yet frightened from their 'hallow'd haunt' (137-8) by Bethlehem's 'dreaded Infant'.

# 4

# A Caustic Masque

What we call *Comus* did not get that name till 1738 when John Dalton restyled it for the 18th-century stage. Milton called it *A Masque presented at Ludlow Castle, 1634*. Critics have complained that it is more like a lecture than a masque—not enough song, dance and pageantry. A risky line to take: we do not know how sumptuously it was staged or how much music and dance there was. How much would the foreground of our impressions, had we been there that Michaelmas night, have been flooded with the torchlit antics of the 'glistering' beasts, the clumping 'jigs' of the Ludlow tenantry, the 'mincing' figures of the courtiers' 'lighter toes' (951–65)? How long would the dances last? How elaborate were the scenic tableaux—a 'wild wood'; a stately palace, full of 'soft music'; Sabrina with water-nymphs and chariot—agate, azure, emerald; a panorama of Ludlow and its castle? How much ingenuity went into special effects: the Spirit changing in and out of rainbowy 'sky-robes', the dazzling powder Comus flings into the air, the artificial moon turning mock clouds and grove to silver (223–4)? How much was sung? Henry Lawes certainly set parts of the Spirit's closing speeches to music —his copy (with music for some of the songs) survives; and both manuscripts of *Comus* have the direction 'Song ends' in the middle of the Spirit's speech of thanks to Sabrina. The last sixth of *Comus*, from the Sabrina invocation on, was more like opera than play, and the varied tempos of Comus's first speech (93–144) suggest that had musical setting as well.

Still Milton, unlike most masque-writers, loads his gilded receptacle with a pair of debates—between the brothers, and between Comus and the Lady. Most people find them undramatic, especially the first, and the rejoinder that a masque was not *meant* to be dramatic cannot get over the fact that it was not meant to be boring either. Johnson's dissatisfaction has been properly echoed: 'So far as the action is merely human, it ought to be reasonable'—by 'reasonable' he meant close to what would be expected in life. Why do the brothers leave their sister alone? Why do they talk so much? 'When they have feared lest their sister should be in danger, and hoped that she is not in danger, the Elder makes a speech in praise of chastity, and the Younger finds how fine it is to be a philosopher.'

Johnson's first question strikes at the root of the action—the separation of this Eve from her protecting Adams. It can be countered on his own naturalistic ground. He forgets that the boys, Viscount Brackley and his brother, were only little: one eleven, the other nine. But their sister was fifteen, and enough of a young woman to occupy the centre of a masque about chastity. Given that she was tired out, and someone had to find food (182–7), neither of the smaller children could be expected to set off into the dark wood by himself. They still believed in ghosts and goblins (434–6): Lady Alice had the willpower to dismiss such 'fantasies' (205). Milton's insight goes further: at the dawn of womanhood new problems inevitably draw a girl away from the confidence of her brothers. Allegory seconds Lady Alice's loneliness.

Certainly naturalism will not help to defend the brothers' loitering, though. They do not behave like real-life boys, and if Johnson seems to be confusing art and life by requiring that they should, it has to be granted that the degree of realism is inconsistent within the masque itself. The brothers' smash and grab raid (813–14) accelerates to the lifelike, and so condemns by contrast their earlier leisureliness. Internal contradiction of this sort was probably even more acute in the acted version, though here, as with the music and dancing, we are more or less in the dark. *Comus* is strictly a lost work. Before our 1645 printed version came the 1637 edition, supervised by Lawes, and there are two manuscripts, the Trinity, in Milton's hand, heavily corrected between 1634 and 1645, and the Bridgewater, copied from the Trinity by a professional penman late in 1637. Even the first draft of the Trinity, picked out from under all Milton's crossings-out, is not the original *Comus* but a later transcript. Which version was spoken on Michaelmas night 1634, no one knows. But several bits that sound energetic and dramatic in the Jacobean manner got cut from the Trinity manuscript during revision. After a placid beginning (407–9), for instance, the Elder Brother flared up: 'Beshrew me, but I would, though now i' th' dark, try/A tough passado with the shaggiest ruffian/That lurks by hedge or lane of this dead circuit/To have her by my side.' The first phrase was quickly toned down to 'I could be willing', and the fencing-jargon—'passado'—gave way to the more staid 'encounter'. By 1637 the lines had been thrown overboard altogether, and the speech continued on the unruffled note of its opening. The same brother's determination to 'cleave' Comus's 'scalp/Down to the hips' (607–8) was moderated to pulling his hair and killing him later. As Milton blotted out the dashing moments, stiffening the fabric of his work, he smoothed away contradictions of pace which must have made the level of realism in the acted version even more irregular than in the one Johnson read.

Clearly a dramatist may disrupt his level of realism. Johnson, in his sternness with the unnatural brothers, has not looked far enough for Milton's motives. Different literary genres are differently separable from their social contexts. The masque's separability is minimal. Designed for a single occasion and particular, non-professional actors whose relationship with the select audience is known and exploitable, its final form is not print but the irrecoverable, intimate spectacle of its first night. Some of the social interplay which went to the making of *Comus* we can still sense. Twice compliments are paid to Henry Lawes, the children's music-teacher (84–9, 494–6): in the second the elder brother speaks; in the first Lawes, who played the part of Thyrsis, has to praise himself in front of pupils and parents. Is Milton being gently mischievous? Exactly what note would be struck? We notice, too, that of the three children only Lady Alice is entrusted with a song, earning extravagant applause (designedly overdone?) from her tutor (555–62). But Comus is struck by the Lady's song, too; and Sabrina's singing—and chastity—are important in the resolution. We do not know who took these parts, so cannot begin to rejoin the threads between actor, role and hearers. Time has rubbed away the identity of the 'shepherd lad', too, so explicitly described by Thyrsis (619–28)—does his knowledge of 'healing herbs' point to Diodati, the medical student: was he known to Lawes and the Egertons? At all events, the relationship between children and parents was the commanding factor in the social context on this occasion, and for Milton to overlook it would have been a major blunder, whereas the consistent realism expected by Johnson was altogether immaterial to him. To persuade the Earl of Bridgewater and his wife that their children were lost and worried was not possible or desirable. What they wanted to know was that their sons were (as Lawes carefully explains) educated as befitted their station— 'nurs't in Princely lore'. Hence the elder boy's virtuous verbosity, including an accurate paraphrase (464–75) of a section from Plato's *Phaedo*, and the younger's pious distinction between himself and the 'dull fools' who do not find philosophy charming. The critic who objects to lost children behaving so collectedly may plead realism, but is himself the reverse of realistic, respond-ing to the fictional situation—two lost children—but ignoring the real—two little noblemen gravely showing off before proud parents. Piping their precocious lines, or brandishing their miniature swords, they were designed to appeal to the indulgent humour of a devoted household, arousing tenderness and laughter —the latter, particularly, with mock-artlessness: 'To tell thee sadly, Shepherd, without blame,/Or our neglect, we lost her as we came' (509–10)—and blending them into a pleasure special to this masque and its context.

These excuses may seem to trivialise a work which shows signs of taking itself seriously. Surely *Comus* was not merely an opportunity for parents to simper over their children? We know that chastity, the doctrinal marrow of the masque, figured importantly at this time in Milton's plans for being an epic poet. Can the levity in his treatment of the boys be squared with a didactic impetus in the whole? That private experience which Milton provided for the Egerton household, with its special shades and tones, has vanished. But the loving first-night audience may, by its very closeness, have been blinded to snags which trouble an objective eye. Milton, so far as we know, was not particularly attached to the Egertons. They employed his friend, Lawes, to teach music. The children's grandmother had a big house at Harefield, near Horton, and the previous summer Milton had written part of an entertainment (*Arcades*) for them to act there. There is no reason to suppose that these aristocratic children would be sacrosanct to a high-minded middle-class intellectual. The first audience was complacent enough for any implied criticism to pass over its heads. But without turning *Comus* into a warren of 'ironies', it is possible to ask some simple questions about what is said and done, and end up with the conviction that if the watchers on Michaelmas night 1634 scanned one facet of Milton's purpose with eager approval, another went, for that reason, uninspected.

This brings us, naturally, to Comus and the Lady: a worrying pair, to most readers. Comus seems so healthy and energetic, the Lady so negative. That most people are readers is half the trouble. We forget that Lady Alice (a portrait survives) was extremely pretty—big dark eyes ('love-darting', Comus calls them) and a pert little mouth. The sexlessness of print neutralises the experience of seeing this delicate creature exposed before an audience and having to hear her virginity discussed by a man—a titillation quite beyond the scope of the public stage, where female roles were still taken by boys. But if the original audience would be less disposed to criticise the Lady, and more alert to the delicious contrast between her appearance and opinions, that is not to say that Milton's presentation of her subsides into the simplicity of an 'ideal'. Her aristocratic assumptions about the morals and manners of the agricultural working class strike coldly, and Milton slyly punishes her. She comes in talking about the 'rudeness and swill'd insolence' of 'loose unletter'd Hinds' (174–8), but conveniently changes her tune when she meets a shepherd, and assures him that it is surprising

45

how often people from his background turn out to be courteous (321–6). Her indignation (691–4) when she discovers that the supposed shepherd was also insincere at the interview borders on the laughable. Further, because she is patently satisfied about her own social elevation, the arguments for financial equality (768–79) which she resorts to in answer to Comus have a hollow ring. The middle of an elaborately-mounted masque is hardly the place to start preaching against luxury: the form betrays how comfortably theoretical the distribution of excessive wealth was likely to remain. And should Lady Alice really have been taken in by the cottager's cringing description of her brothers—'more than human', 'a fäery vision', 'gay creatures of the element/That in the colours of the Rainbow live' (297–300)? No doubt the little lads looked dapper enough—a bill for their masquing costumes is among the scraps that have survived, and Milton acidly notes their resemblance to the self-admiring Narcissus (237)—but what Comus is reckoning on, rather, and quite justifiably as it turns out, is an upper-class ear well dulled by flattery.

The Lady's class-prejudices, however, do not occupy the centre of our attention, and would presumably have seemed altogether natural to the audience. But there are other elements in the masque which suggest some spiritual deficiency. She does, after all, get glued to Comus's chair, and the chair 'Smear'd with gums of glutinous heat' (917) brings to mind the sexual heat for which Comus's enchantments are allegories. Sabrina has to come with 'chaste' palms (918) to unglue her. Yet, according to the Elder Brother, the girl who has chastity is immune against physical assault ('clad in complete steel' 421) and 'may pass on with unblench't majesty' (430). Lady Alice cannot 'pass on'; or even get up to go. The proviso which he adds, 'Be it not done in pride or in presumption' (431), raises doubts. Is it the Lady's pride that makes her physically helpless against Comus? Does her confidence that heaven will send a 'glist'ring Guardian' to protect her (219–20) amount to 'presumption'? The Elder Brother believes also that 'Virtue could see to do what virtue would/By her own radiant light', even if sun and moon were extinguished (373–4). This does not tally with his sister's complaints about the darkness

(195–200), or her bewilderment in the 'blind mazes' of the wood where her 'best guide' is her ear (170–82), or with the success of Comus's dust in cheating her eye with 'blear illusion' (155). And though Viscount Brackley is confident that when heaven finds a sincerely chaste soul 'A thousand liveried Angels lackey her,/Driving far off each thing of sin and guilt', no angels drive Comus away when he approaches Lady Alice. In each case, is the brother mistaken or the sister less than completely virtuous? Readers usually take his long Spenserian-Platonic pronouncements (359–85, 418–75) at face value, but is it possible to do so without turning the masque into an exposure of Lady Alice's inadequacies so pointed as to make it unpalatable to her parents, unless they were too besotted to notice what was going on? Alternatively the brother may be hopelessly idealistic in his suppositions about chastity: this would fit in with the half-humorous presentation of the boys, and make his speeches, in the context of the whole, unserious. A further way out of the dilemma is to explain the Elder Brother's confident arguments as a ruse to cheer up the smaller boy. Knowing the real danger himself, he throws together a few highflown notions as a make-shift shelter for his junior. This reading of the text finds encouragement in the Younger Brother's earlier tendency to panic, and his generally weaker grasp of issues. His idea of the higher life consists of everlasting sweets with no risk of stomach-ache (479–80); and by comparing his sister's beauty to a 'Miser's treasure' (399) he concedes a view of the affair which fits better with Comus's ('Beauty is nature's coin, must not be hoarded' 739) than with the Lady's. The Elder Brother's jumpiness—his philosophic calm comically upset by a sudden shout (480) just as he has managed to talk the smaller boy round—may also indicate that he has little faith in what he has been saying.

As to Lady Alice's spiritual perfections, then, *Comus* ventures a question-mark. Maybe her eventual gluey predicament implies shortcomings, or maybe, despite her brother's claims, virtue and chastity can free the mind only, not the body. Either way Sabrina seems best interpreted as a symbol of divine grace extended to sinful flesh. The Spirit applies the word 'grace' to her activities (938), and her triple sprinkling recalls baptism and the Trinity (911-15).

A strict interpretation of the action raises uncomfortable questions about the brothers, too. Though provided with haemony (638) they fail to secure Comus's wand as instructed (653). 'What, have you let the false enchanter scape?' (814) complains the Spirit. To adopt so grumbling a tone would hardly be fair unless the boys had a real chance of success. The indirectness of the Spirit's earlier behaviour—why did he not rescue the girl himself instead of going off to find the brothers?—seems accountable only as the purposeful involvement of the younger children in a test complementary to their sister's. They fail it. Their sister's temptation—the enchanted cup—Milton borrowed from Homer's *Odyssey* where the cup of Circe (Comus's mother) turns Odysseus's men to animals, and where he is given a herb, moly (compared with haemony by the Spirit, 636), which makes him proof against her charms. Christian interpreters had allegorised Circe as lust; her conflict with Odysseus as passion against reason; moly as temperance. 'As Circe's rod, waved over their heads from the right side to the left, presents those false and sinister persuasions of pleasure which so much deforms them, so the reversion thereof, by discipline and a view of their own deformity, restores them to their former beauties', wrote Sandys, one of Milton's favourite mythographers. The brothers, missing the wand, leave Comus's followers sub-human. Maybe this means nothing more damaging to them than that 'discipline and a view of their own deformity' were things beyond the power of a nine- and eleven-year-old to bring to the Ludlow revellers welcoming the Earl of Bridgewater, or perhaps a darker reflection upon the ruling class could be deduced. Here, too, we are in a region of question-marks which the masque's first audience would hardly have explored.

Once we start looking, other question-marks spring up. Haemony seems a needlessly obscure symbol, if it is a symbol, and the concerted labours of critics have left it indefinite. Coleridge, however, breaking it into two Greek words meaning 'blood' and 'wine', gave it sacramental suggestions which seem hard to resist, particularly in view of Sabrina and 'grace'. The pagan temperance ('moly') needs succour, we conclude, from the communion table. Haemony's 'prickles' (631) recall the crown of thorns; its 'bright golden flow'r' borne only in 'another Country' (632–3), the crown of glory. 'In this soil', though, it is 'Unknown, and like esteem'd', trodden underfoot by dull swains (634–5). This does not say much for the spiritual state of Wales and the Marches, or of Ludlow Castle. Similarly the Spirit's opening description of the earth as a cattle-pound ('pinfold'), a 'dim spot' full of 'smoke and stir' (5), casts doubt upon his view of the British Isles, the next moment, as 'rich and various gems' (22). The 'old and haughty Nation proud in Arms' (33), which appears when he starts distributing bouquets, has been surprisingly produced out of 'Confin'd and pester'd', 'frail and Feverish' humans, 'Unmindful of the crown that Virtue gives' (7–9). Socrates, in Plato's *Phaedo*, had said that what men lived on, and thought to be the earth's surface ('this dim spot,/Which men call Earth'), was really made up of damp, dark hollows: the earth's true surface lay far above, 'In Regions mild of calm and serene Air'. The Spirit's Platonism knocks the bottom out of his compliments. The same can be said of Milton's elevation of virginity in a masque which was meant to congratulate the Earl and his wife on their 'fair offspring'. Family life and sexual abstinence do not blend happily, and the Earl, who had fifteen children in all, might have reasons as insistent as Comus's for doubting 'the sage/And serious doctrine of Virginity' (786–7). Also, though it probably did not strike the Ludlow audience, when Comus counsels the outraged Lady to show off her beauty 'In courts, at feasts, and high solemnities' (746), he describes what she is already doing by performing in the masque. Comus's excitement about staying up after dark to dance (102–22) involves all the Michaelmas-night dancers at Ludlow. 'We that are of purer fire/Imitate the Starry Choir', though addressed to the beast-headed rout, brings the Lady, her brothers and the audience into Comus's territory. The 'mirth and cheer' (955), dancing and 'Court guise' (962) of the splendid and numerous company (948–9) at the President's Castle sound

49

more like Comus's 'Joy and Feast' (102)—not to mention his 'Tipsy dance and Jollity' (104)—than the Lady's 'spare Temperance' (767). Her speech at entrance, 'This is the place, as well as I may guess,/Whence ev'n now the tumult of loud Mirth/Was rife and perfect in my list'ning ear' (201–3), strikes beyond its dramatic context to the hall in which she is standing. It would not take a very jaundiced spectator to see Comus as presiding deity of the Ludlow festivities (his name in Greek means 'a merrymaking'), or Milton's as a masque against masquing. Comus's power over the Lady, and the brothers' ill-success against him, may both reflect the taint of their performance and of the values it implies.

An aspect of the masque which has proved more commonly disappointing is the unexciting climax. Here, naturally, Milton was hampered by circumstances. His current theories made him interested in chastity and the perils it faced, but rape is a delicate subject to dramatise in front of your leading lady's parents. Early on, the brothers talk promisingly enough about their sister 'within the direful grasp/Of Savage hunger or of Savage heat' (357–8), and Comus, thinking along the same lines, fancies the Lady as his 'Queen' (265). But decency prevails, and the threat peters out into symbolic action. All that happens is that the Lady gets offered a drink. Comus, besides, cannot be said to go about it with any skill. Sticking your guest to a chair is not the likeliest way to persuade her to accept hospitality, particularly when you let her see beforehand the effect your refreshments have had on previous visitors. Lady Alice knows that Comus has put something in her drink ('Hence with thy brew'd enchantments' 696), and would have to be half-witted to accept it. The action does not remotely suggest the way chastity gets tempted in life, where the essence of the situation is that the girl wants to be loved by her tempter.

A further weakness which develops from the change of direction is that, though Comus's argument eventually arrives at some conventional advice about rose-plucking, its most impressive phase bears no relation to what had seemed the matter in hand. Its very intensity and scope drag it away from the limited but vital issue: whether the Lady will surrender her body. Speculations about an increase in bird population, for example, however magnificently pictured (730), are lavishly beside the point. It would be expedient to explain these plausible irrelevancies as part of Comus's cunning. But the Lady contents herself with replying on the same distant level, instead of switching the debate indignantly back to her own intimate concerns. Even at her closest approach to the sexual question she stays in the area of impersonal polemic, naming virginity as a 'doctrine' (787), not a fact of her own body. The ground of discussion is thus cautiously shifted to a broad allegorical plane—temperance versus intemperance—which purports to include but actually curtains off the urgent physiological predicament of threatened virginity. To recall Isabella confronting Angelo or Claudio in *Measure for Measure* is to get some idea of the consequent loss.

Still, it is not so much a matter of allegory being an inadequate mode as of Milton's being an inadequate allegory—dangerously so, by fostering belief in tempters who untemptingly mishandle their advantages. A way out is to offer Milton's allegory as a representation not of temptation but flat rejection. But even disregarding the questionable value of rejection unprefaced by inner debate, a reader might have misgivings about the Lady's superiority over the figure she rejects. Comus's praise of Nature (706–36) exhibits an imaginative response far richer than the Lady's. Her reply, labouring under a crude moral vocabulary, bespeaks an almost metallic insensitivity ('I had not thought to have unlockt my lips') which reduces Nature to a 'good cateress' (764), and earth to a 'brute' (797). Her explanation that she is not really trying (793) does little to alleviate the effect of stolidity. Of course, the contrast is to some degree calculated. Reason stays close to the ground while Passion performs on the high-wire. Noticeably the Lady talks in Comus's poetic language only once, when fear momentarily quells her reason, producing the famous lines about 'airy tongues that syllable men's names/On Sands and Shores and desert Wildernesses' (208–9). Reason, though, if drably unprovided with sensuous imagination, ought to score with its arguments. The flaws in Comus's logic offer plain targets. He infers from natural plenty a being, Nature, who intends man's enjoyment (710–20). 17th-century thinking about nature could make short work of such hopeful animism, but the Lady, instead of exposing his method, accepts it. Her appeal to a 'most innocent Nature' who intends her 'children' to be temperate (762–7) is equally baseless. Again, Comus assumes that people who lived on vegetables and water would not thank the 'all-giver' (720–3). The Lady adopts a reverse position just as naïve by supposing that gluttonous people never say grace (776–9). Further, her proposal that nature's blessings should be evenly distributed (768–73), carrying with it the admission that enjoyment is preferable to abstinence, concedes Comus's point (706–9). Altogether her rejoinder, instead of effecting a realignment of the issues, seems a bewildered reaction to superior cleverness. Hotly aware of her opponent's falsity, she is unable to pin it down, and falls back on the lame assertion that he is too depraved to understand the truth (784–9). Intellectual address seems Comus's prerogative, as well as imaginative vivacity. Theoretically the Lady is so much in the right that her words make him sweat and tremble, a result unlikely enough on the face of it for Milton to explain vaguely that they are 'set off by some superior power' (801); but it is hard to see how, if she really represented any kind of rightness, it could profit from association with slow wit and misdirected argument. Previous hints of imperfection in Lady Alice come to mind, and her conduct in the debate widens the rift between heroine and ideal. Meanwhile her nominal victory presumably reassured friends in the audience.

The young gentlemen, their haughty sister and their opulent home may have struck Milton as frail vehicles for an ideal, but the work he wrote for them has always persuaded readers of its deeply idealistic stamp, and a sensitivity to the critical stings it contains can only strengthen that impression. Lawes, as the Spirit, escapes criticism. Musicians, like philosophers, could give the soul wings to carry it up from the dark world, so the neo-Platonists believed (the Trinity manuscript makes the Spirit a Platonic 'daemon'), and Lawes lives 'Above the smoke and stir'

(5) of earth, descending occasionally, as music teacher, to bring the benighted children harmony. Interpreters in search of the masque's 'message' have naturally scrutinised Lawes's closing speech, encouraged by the rewriting of lines 976–1023 in the Trinity manuscript and the later addition of lines 1000–1011 which, along with 'List mortals, if your ears be true' (997), make it look as if Milton took pains to get the speech right. Venus ('th' Assyrian Queen'), watching over Adonis in a garden, inevitably discloses behind Milton's lines the garden of Adonis from Spenser's *Faerie Queene* where all life, human, animal, vegetable, originates. For the Renaissance mythographer Adonis was a sun-symbol, nourisher of seeds—the idea goes back at least to the Orphic *Hymn to Adonis* (4th century); the boar which wounds him was winter; Venus, the earth. The identifications came so familiarly to Milton that in his early verses *On the Death of a Fair Infant* winter, killing the little girl, gets two lines (6–7) which belong to the boar in Shakespeare's *Venus and Adonis*. The sun-and-earth figures in Lawes's speech are the lovers who parted so shamefacedly in the *Nativity Ode* ('It was no season then for her/To wanton with the Sun, her lusty Paramour'). As agents of reproductive love their role need not be disgraceful —though Comus is a follower of Venus (124) and grandson of Adonis (51). But they are firmly subordinated to the divine pair, 'Celestial Cupid' and Psyche, 'far above'. Psyche's name means 'soul', and celestial Love who is also the 'fam'd son' of earth can only be the Son of Man. The scene unfolds with unwavering orthodoxy as the marriage of the Lamb, from *Revelation* xxi, with the New Jerusalem ('the bride, the Lamb's wife'), home of those 144,000 virgin souls from *Revelation* xiv which had so engaged the young Milton's attention, as he admits in the *Apology*. Hence the oath 'Jove' is said to have 'sworn' about Cupid and Psyche's children (in Spenser and classical tradition they had only a daughter, Pleasure): Youth ('Behold, I make all things new') and Joy ('God shall wipe away all tears from their eyes') are the promises of the voice from heaven John hears in *Revelation* xxi. Christianity and Platonism blend. Virtue and, as the masque's constant emphasis implies,

virginity, will teach you to soar up through the musical spheres (1019–21), and at the top you will find yourself in the *Book of Revelation*.

But *Comus* can so evidently not be allegorised away into a biblical nook that the last speech seems less a conclusion than a diversion. True, the dark wood shows signs all along of being the wicked wood of life, in which Dante found himself at the start of the *Divine Comedy*—only 'prosperous' to Comus (270): the others call it 'drear', 'ominous', 'a dungeon' and 'hideous'. But Lady Alice despite, or because of, her uppishness and blunders becomes more humanly considerable than a virgin-psyche-symbol. Besides, she looked sure to attract a husband (and did), so moved in a warmer climate than the masque's lifelong virgins, Sabrina, Diana (441), Minerva (448). Milton's treatment of her brothers, now genial, now severe, entails a livelier commerce with life than the earth-escaping drive of the *Nativity Ode* and *Il Penseroso* would have sanctioned. The masque, equipped both to engage the Ludlow merrymakers and to question their complacencies, appears faceted and inclusive beside the earlier poems. And Comus—vital, passionate, Satanically responsive to beauty ('Sure something holy lodges in that breast' 246), deeply corrupt, yet capable of 'sacred' delight (262), and pathetically eager to enlarge his horrible collection (151–3), is a creation unequalled in Milton's previous writing. His poetry wears a Shakespearean fabric of metaphor, constantly depending on the junction of unlikely elements—fish morris-dancing (115–16), a raven smiling (251–2), worms keeping shops (715–16)—and finds its climax in the melting of natural boundaries, as subterranean creatures rise into sunlight (734–6). Typically he unthreads joints (614). His rout confounds human and animal. Comus embodies the unifying charge of poetic language. He is a growth of the passionate life that Milton had tried to throttle in Elegy 6 and the *Nativity Ode*. His riotous sociability would clog the epic aspirant's wings, and Milton fiercely brutalises it, but his poetic fluency cannot be resisted.

# 5

# Evading death: *Lycidas*

On 10 August 1637 Edward King, a Fellow of Christ's, four years Milton's junior, was drowned on his way to Ireland from Chester. There had been 'a particular friendship and intimacy' between him and Milton, or so Milton's nephew says, and when King's friends got together a book of memorial verse, *Lycidas* was the last and longest English contribution. Posterity has doubted the intimacy: the poem holds itself so artificially. The *Epitaph for Damon* (i.e. Diodati), written in 1640, brings back the lost hours with a familiarity that never quite enters the earlier poem: Milton sits up late talking with Diodati while roasted pears and nuts hiss and crackle on the grate, and the night wind thunders through the elms. *Lycidas* wheels a screen of artifice around such moments: it is difficult to imagine what Milton and King were up to behind the sheep and the satyrs (23–36). Not that artifice stagnates the poem. The intricate verse, Milton's most elaborate recasting of the Italian forms, the anger, the questioning, bear out the alertness of his 'eager thought' (189) and the strictness of the poet's 'trade' (65). What suffers is our appetite for vicarious emotion. Grief cannot keep its sharpness in the classical air. Totting up the debts to Theocritus, Moschus and Virgil merely makes the grief seem second-hand. Tremulous moments do survive—'Weep no more, woeful shepherds, weep no more' (165) would have the stoniest shepherd reaching for his handkerchief—but the poem mostly seems too preoccupied for tears, and the uncouth swain twitching his mantle free and making off (192) looks improperly cheerful. Immediacy of event is lacking, too. Hopkins gives more information in two lines—'On Saturday sailed from Bremen,/American-outward-bound'—than Milton does in his whole poem. When *Lycidas* was reprinted it had to have a headnote explaining the subject. Circumstances of the wreck—King kneeling in prayer while the other passengers milled about the deck—get into the memorial volume elsewhere, but are shut out of Milton's offering. The repulsiveness of drowning is only intermittently conveyed. Water 'clos'd' (it has a sinister gentleness) over Lycidas's head (51); the body is said to 'welter to the parching wind' (13). Bloated, we imagine, and dried on top. But 'bones' being 'hurl'd' (155) supply a different image. The sheep rotting inwardly, 'swoln with wind' (126), are more consistently imagined. Perhaps only 'wat'ry floor' (167) creates the right alarm: deceptively firm from above, an imprisoning fact for the drowning man beneath.

Some people find the poem's very evasiveness moving—the inhibitions suggested by the 'tender stops' (if it is not perverse to see ambiguity here), on which it is played (188). A sense of what it can by no means bring itself to face stands darkly behind its dallying with 'false surmise' (153). It seems uneasy with self-deception ('Ay me, I fondly dream', 56), but plucks its 'quills' and 'oaten pipes' from the *Shepherd's Calendar*, and prattles, like the *Calendar* swains, in rustic forms ('daffadillies') and dialect ('rathe', 'scrannel'). Even the two passages in which a 'higher mood' breaks free of pastoral (76–84, 113–31) preserve the pastoral mannerisms and do not look squarely at King's death but aside at Milton's anxiety about his own fame and the future of the Church of England.

To be affected by the poem's escapism will seem weakness to readers convinced of its frigidity. But Milton's lapse into the arms of Flora and old Pan can hardly, considering his earlier poetry, be reduced to classicism. His imaginative hunger for an invisibly peopled landscape, 'the gentle neighbourhood of grove and spring', was frustrated by King's death in the 'remorseless deep'. Fiction began to collapse. *Lycidas* hopefully repairs the damage. After accusing the nymphs of neglect (50), then doubting their power (57), it stages a court of enquiry (the legal setting supplied by 'plea', 'felon' and 'dungeon') at which, under examination, the god of winds reveals that 'not a blast' blew at the time of the wreck (97), and that the nymphs did keep the sea calm (98–9). Since the verses in the memorial volume by King's brother specifically mention an 'unlucky storm', it looks as if Milton had to discard the facts before building King's death into his poem at all. The wind-god vaguely blames the ship, with some hints about black magic remembered from *Macbeth*. The next witness, a river god, has no idea who was responsible for King's death. Nor, more worryingly, has the mitred figure who follows (named loosely enough to be either St. Peter or Christ). The implication that even he wanted to save King (113), along with Phoebus's tacit admission that death, if not fame, is the work of a 'blind Fury' (75), looses anarchy upon the poem's world, against which the bland announcement that King is not dead after all sounds like equivocation. He is dead, and the poem, for all its trying, does not explain why.

The nature gods inevitably seem separate from St. Peter, Christ and a thinly-disguised 'all-judging Jove' (82). Hence *Lycidas*'s tendency to split. The split is worsened by Milton's twice calling himself lengthily to heel (85–8, 132–5) after the Christian insertions. And that two directions should so openly be followed even at the end, landing Lycidas both in heaven and on the west coast (174–81, 183–5), threatens the assurance of either. The 'Genius of the shore' might be dismissed as decoration (though not without trivialising the poem's close), but his family connections with the controlling genii of *Arcades* and *Comus* speak for him. Perhaps we should understand that King, like the Attendant Spirit, will return to earth for coastguard duty when necessary, though usually in heaven. But this solution is discouraged by the finality of the Christian 'for ever' (181). The Attendant Spirit lived, less finally, 'before the threshold' of Jove's court.

The transcendent leap of Phoebus's reply, recommending heavenly fame, and of King's ascent to heaven, is contested by the circular movements of nature. Critics eager to find vestiges of fertility rites may have ridden the nature-cycles too hard, but that does not remove them from the poem. The evergreens, carrying life through the winter, but shattered 'before the mellowing year' (5), the flowers nipped by early frosts (47) but later flashing into colour and abundance (142–50), bind the poem to a wheel. King's death at the height of summer (10 August) may allow a sentimental interpretation of the 1637 autumn (42–4), but the poem has to admit that the seasons rotate with no care for man: only 'false surmise' can sign on the 1638 spring flowers as mourners. The understandably constant references to water reveal another circle lying beneath the poem. The bitter sea feeds and is fed by sweetness and life. 'Honied' rain revives the flowers; and sheep fatten, surprisingly, on 'fresh dews' (140, 29). But the brooks, gushing along their 'fresh' valleys (136–8), make for the sea with 'swift' Hebrus, 'Smooth-sliding' Mincius and Camus 'footing' reluctantly to death (103). Lycidas, who has to be snatched from nature's whirl, washes his salty hair in 'Nectar', and has his salt tears wiped away (175, 181). But placing him, apparently for good, among 'other groves, and other streams' (174), and making even heavenly fame a 'plant' (78), unsettlingly returns him to the pattern that groves and streams obey. The sun traces a third circle; rising and sinking over the undergraduate shepherds (25–31), sinking and rising to take Lycidas into heaven (168–72). But the sun poised 'in the forehead of the morning sky' (171) symbolises impermanence, not stability, and makes the point by dropping, with Lycidas, back to the Irish Sea before the poem ends (191). Amaranthus (149), the immortal flower of paradise, being told to shed its beauty with the real flowers, contributes on its own small scale to this shaking of what purports to be permanence.

*Lycidas*'s struggle towards Christian transcendence is compellingly challenged, then, by a more basic consolation which merges the single death into a leafy background of growth and decay. The fertility-heroes who more or less questionably frequent the poem (Hyacinth, who died a boy and rose a flower, comes clearly into view (106), and lingers behind the 'Crow-toe' (143)—wild hyacinth; Adonis and Attis, from whose blood sprung rose and violet (45, 145), may pass fleetingly), throw what weight they have behind the seasonal rhythm.

So does Orpheus. Nature's lament for King (39–41) is nature's lament for Orpheus in Ovid, and Orpheus's head floating to Lesbos (63–4) suggests King's 'sacred head' (51, 102)—'divine head' was an earlier reading in the Orpheus passage (62). Probably Milton knew from Selden about the papyrus head of Adonis which was thrown into the sea at Alexandria each year, and taken out at Byblos as a token of the reborn sun-god. His own sun's 'drooping head' rises renewed from the water. The ritual of immersion relates to a cylic, not an arrested process, and though the poem pretends to resurrect Orpheus–King once and for all, the unknown Orpheus singing to 'Oaks and rills' (186), as Lycidas had to willows and hazels, sets the wheel turning again.

The Christian claim to eternity (172–81) is valiantly, it can be argued, still there. Flowers, sun and sea stir a vortex that, far from engulfing it, throws it clear. But other features of the poem thicken the doubt. When, for example, the last speaker at the enquiry seems bent on arresting degeneracy with Christian certainty, he falters. His two-handed engine, smothered beneath scholarly dispute—is it the sword of God, the sword of Michael, the axe of *Matthew* iii, the sheep hook, the shears, England and Scotland, the Houses of Parliament, or what?—has only its own vagueness to blame. Even to pronounce it more terrifying for its mystery is to grant that here the thread of assertion frays.

There is also something unclear about the tenses of the poem. The singer starts in the present—'I come' (3)—and asks questions —'What boots it?' and so on—as matters of present concern. But the past tense 'Phoebus repli'd' (77) oddly indicates an earlier answer. Similarly the court of enquiry, with Hippotades' explanation that nature was not to blame and the mitred figure's promise of retribution, is phrased in the past tense, implying it took place before the song we are listening to began. Why, then, does the singer still ask questions ('Where were ye Nymphs?', 'Were it not better done?') which have been answered? The tense-changes can hardly be an oversight. The usual account is that they emphasise the poem's artificiality, its status as performance; but they could equally be seen as disrupting the artifice. And does not the perseverance of questions after answers have been given cast a doubt upon the answers? Considerations of place, as well as time, weaken the effect of the court of enquiry. One witness 'came' (90), another 'went' (103), another 'Last came, and last did go' (108). But where they came to and went from is not shown. The scene, in spite of its firm arrival-and-departure verbs, hangs in the air.

In *Lycidas*, as in *Comus*, fertility collides with chastity. Having to forgo the 'delights' of Amaryllis and Neaera seems a particular grudge. Flowers are prudently supplied with a 'wardrobe' (47)—'buttons' was an earlier version—and wear 'embroidery' (148)—'livery' in the first draft. The woodbine is 'well-attir'd' (146). The singer gathers his skirts around himself before leaving (192). The valley's 'lap' (where 'shades' and 'wanton' suggest Amaryllis) is 'sparely' eyed by the hot dog-star (136–8). The primrose (142), before Milton corrected his draft, died *Winter's-Tale*-ishly 'unwedded . . . Colouring the pale cheek of unenjoyed love'. King's 'nuptial Song' (176) is that at the chaste marriage of the Lamb which ended *Comus* and, with heavier stress on the virginal entrance-fee, ends the *Epitaph for Damon*: 'Diodati . . . because the blush of modesty and a youth without stain were your choice, and because you never tasted the delight of the marriage bed, virginal honours are reserved for you.' King, wiped and washed and laved (155, 175, 181) is, too, lifted from a contaminating 'bed' (168).

The Shakespearean amplitude of the masque's style has ebbed. *Lycidas*'s 'gust of rugged wings' blowing 'from off each beaked Promontory' (93–4) brings to light a cliff-sized bird, to match Comus's creative metaphors. Usually, though, the verbal life is less vivid: 'leaves' (5), in the apology for premature publication, thinly evoke book as well as tree; and there is only a ghost of Pegasus beneath Fame's 'spur' (70). True, the supernatural figures are sometimes translated into water-pastoral brilliantly. 'Through the dear might of him that walk'd the waves' (173) springs Christ on us in a movingly appropriate role; Atropos is cast as a hideously incompetent, blind sheep-shearer (75–6). But decorativeness can jumble the images. 'My destin'd Urn' (20) implies cremation; 'my sable shroud' (22), burial. Shrouds, anyway, were white: Milton's 'sable shroud' became a favourite bit of poetic diction. Occasionally a self-conscious sprightliness governs the words: 'Blind mouths' (119) are complemented by 'eyes' that 'suck' (139–40). The idea seems to get out of hand: 'Blind mouths! that scarce themselves know how to hold/A Sheep-hook'. Would even an incompetent shepherd hold one in his mouth? But perhaps the ridiculous image is reckoned on, and perhaps the incongruous associations of 'wat'ry bier' and 'meed' (12–14) and of 'Keys' and 'Mitred locks' (110–12) are as well. It seems more plausible that Milton has given his diction, at these points, a life which shoves at the surrounding decorousness, than that he has missed the connections. After all, the poem was written for a book of fashionably witty tributes.

Verbal playfulness is left behind by the power-driven lines which speculate on the body's whereabouts—'Whether beyond the stormy Hebrides' and so on to the sleep of the Cornish giants and 'the great vision of the guarded Mount' keeping watch on Spain (156–62). Readers who have no ideas about Namancos or Bayona respond to the quickening energies of this poetry. Partly we react to that geographical excitement which could always captivate Milton, but more particularly Lycidas has here become, like Comus, a poetic medium for enrolling experiences nature keeps remote: the storm-surrounded islands, the armed apparition, the buried denizens of a 'monstrous world' that Comus raised. Milton's imagination is at last gripped by King's predicament: the 'hurl'd' corpse, the 'sounding' seas, the 'whelming' tide come crashing through the tissue of artifice. Shakespeare is not far off: 'humming' for 'whelming' in the first draft shows that Thaisa's bitumened coffin sweeping its living occupant beneath the waves was in Milton's mind. With a real corpse, not a mock-shepherd, he has found a way of projecting himself into his creature's experience, of writing with what, in Shakespeare and Keats, would be called 'empathy'. That, too, is what Comus found with his silkworms in 'green shops' and fish dancing a 'wavering morris' to the moon. It is a mode of writing that grapples the artist to the earth, and so in Milton it, like his heroic dream, repeatedly runs up against the other, renunciatory.

# 6

# Writing Left-handed: The Prose Years

The majority of Milton's writing is never read. It consists of prose 'pamphlets' (we should call most of them books), turned out between 1641 and 1660, in which he let it be known that bishops should be abolished (these were, according to his own classification of his prose, the pamphlets on religious liberty); that divorce should be easier and the press free (domestic liberty); and that kings, particularly Charles I, could be rightly beheaded (civil liberty).

Prose was a job for his left hand, said Milton. Later critics have paid their respects to its 'noble periods' and 'racy invective', and used it to illustrate Milton's gradual 'disenchantment' with the monarchy, the people of England, and so forth. This approach entails some naïvety. Propaganda is not the likeliest mirror of a writer's inner self. It is true that the early (anti-bishop) pamphlets are sometimes heatedly royalist, but this was to outmanoeuvre the 'No bishop, no king' alarmists on the other side. Milton can be heard trying out his vocabulary on 'the floting carcas of a crazie and diseased Monarchy' as early as 1641. He was temperamentally anti-monarchic; scornful of 'pomp', and too much of an intellectual not to see the fatuity of hereditary kingship (as if 'the race of Kings were eminently the best of men, as the breed at Tutburie is of Horses'). He hated authority; he was enraged by the authority of inferiors. His demand for a republic, *The Ready and Easy Way to Establish a Free Commonwealth* (1660), was not the outcome of any disenchantment but the rationalisation of what he had always felt.

Too much can be made, too, of Milton's 'patriotic optimism' in the early 1640s. If being a patriot means respecting one's countrymen, Milton was never a patriot. He is shrewd enough to mix in some appeals to 'our deare Mother England', and gratifies his public in *Areopagitica* (1644) by advising the 'Lords and Commons of England' that they are in charge of a nation 'not beneath the reach of any point the highest that human capacity can soar to'. But even here he limits himself to what the English might be like: what they were really like he had told Parliament the previous year—'degenerat and fal'n . . . rushing to whordoms and adulteries'.

It was his constant belief that most men are 'weakly, or falsly principl'd' and when he agitated for liberty, it meant liberty for himself. This is plain even in *Areopagitica*. He wrote it because he had been refused a licence for his first divorce tract. In its grandest moments the personal strain can still be heard. 'Give me the liberty to know, to utter, and to argue freely according to conscience, above all liberties'. Stress the 'me', and the grandeur vanishes; yet this stress does not misrepresent the pamphlet's interests. It is quite content that other authors should be suppressed. 'No law', it takes it for granted, 'can possibly permit' anything 'impious or evil absolutely either against faith or maners' (as if there were no difficulty about applying such terms), and it includes all Roman Catholic writing under this embargo. It calls down 'sharpest justice', 'the fire and the executioner', on 'scandalous, seditious and libellous Books'. 'They who most loudly clamour for liberty,' observes Dr. Johnson in his *Life of Milton*, 'do not most liberally grant it.' *Areopagitica* had no effect on the Long Parliament's licensing policy, and in 1651 Milton himself became a licenser.

Milton's small regard for those of different make-up from himself is well shown by the pamphlet *Of Education*. It consists essentially of a daunting heap of textbooks which the little victims are to devour, 'plying hard, and dayly'. Besides making their way along the various branches of human learning, in Latin, Greek, Hebrew, Aramaic, Syriac and Italian (which 'they may have easily learnt at any odde hour'), they will become proficient in fortification, fencing and wrestling. The need to adapt syllabus to pupil is one that never strikes him. His is the mentality of the conveyor belt. His educational thinking is antediluvian compared with that of the great continental reformer John Comenius (1592–1670), whom Milton scathingly dismisses at the start of his tract. Comenius was already proposing free state education for boys and girls of all classes (Milton's concern is with the sons of 'the nobility and chief gentry'), the exclusion of compulsion and punishment from the classroom (Milton believed in hitting small boys), and the accommodation of methods of instruction to each mind's natural pace and type.

In his onslaught on the bishops, and, later, on the king, it is to Milton's advantage to cry up the rights of the common man, complaining that the public has been treated by its rulers as 'a credulous and hapless herd, begott'n to servility'. When he finds himself opposed by a common man, however, his democracy evaporates. *Colasterion* (1645), the last of his divorce-pamphlets, entertains its readers with the news that one of Milton's opponents is, 'if any can hold laughter, . . . an actual Serving-man'. Milton alludes to him as a 'Pork' and a 'fleamy clodd', objecting to 'the noysom stench of his rude slot', and laboriously explaining the shortcomings in his erudition. When the serving-man, unlike his learned antagonist, worries about what will become of the children of broken marriages, Milton evades the issue with a sneer: 'It must bee good news for Chamber-maids, to hear a Serving-man grown so provident for great bellies.'

Not surprisingly, Milton has nothing to say on behalf of the genuinely progressive democrats: the Levellers, who were demanding the right to vote for all ranks of men over twenty-one, and the Diggers, who claimed that all land must be owned in common. There is no disenchantment with the people, though. They had never enchanted him. Seen in his true colours, Milton is nearer to fascism than to democracy. Answering Salmasius (the scholar hired by the royalists abroad to write against the regicides), he hardly bothers to pretend that the trial and execution of Charles had the support of the English people. He admits that the army was responsible, and praises it for taking matters out of the hands of the majority. The business of securing a majority in Parliament had been simplified on 6 December 1648, when forty-one opposition M.P.s were arrested by the military in the lobby of the House. Milton applauds this way of settling affairs: 'our troops were wiser than our legislators'. In *The Ready and Easy Way* he lays it down as a principle that 'most voices ought not always to prevail, where main matters are in question'. The few with whom Milton agrees will rightly overrule the 'misguided and abused multitude'.

To distrust the 'disenchantment' theory is not to suppose that none of Milton's ideas changed in these twenty years. It seems probable that his trust in the unquestionable authority of the Bible wore thin as he looked more closely into the matter. He had no complaints about the authority of the Bible so long as it did not interfere with what he wished to believe. The anchor of his argument against the bishops is that there is no biblical authority for their existence. He habitually accuses them of 'ridiculous wresting of Scripture', and rejects their emphasis on the obscurity of the Bible as 'a mere suggestion of the Devil to disswade men from reading it'. Within three years, however, we find that he has himself decided that 'there is scarse any one saying in the Gospel but must be read with limitations and distinctions to be rightly understood'. Christ's words are now 'as obscure as any clause fetcht out of Genesis'. The reason for this shift is that in the interim Milton had married, been deserted, and decided that the divorce laws needed attention. This brought him into head-on conflict with Christ, according to most people's interpretation of Scripture.

Milton wanted incompatibility, as well as adultery, to be accepted as grounds for divorce. Both parties should be allowed to remarry. He insisted that divorce was not the business of any court: it was a private matter, which individuals should be allowed to settle for themselves. All the magistrates should concern themselves with was protecting the property rights involved. Moses had said that when a man found 'some uncleanness' in his wife, he should write her a bill of divorcement and send her away. This would leave him free to remarry (*Deutero-*

*nomy* xxiv, 1–2). It was comparatively easy for Milton to make out that the Hebrew word translated 'uncleanness' could mean incompatibility. Much more of an obstacle was Christ's reply to the Pharisees who tried to catch him out, after he had said 'What therefore God hath joined together, let no man put asunder', by quoting Moses' ruling at him:

> He saith unto them, 'Moses because of the hardness of your hearts suffered you to put away your wives: but from the beginning it was not so. And I say unto you, whosoever shall put away his wife, except it be for fornication, and shall marry another, committeth adultery: and whoso marrieth her which is put away doth commit adultery.' MATTHEW xix, 8–9

It is necessary for Milton to explain away Christ's words, or, as he puts it, 'recover their long-lost meaning'. They cannot, he maintains, mean what they say (that remarriage after divorce is equivalent to adultery), because otherwise all the Jews through the ages who had obeyed God's instruction, delivered through Moses, about writing a bill of divorcement and remarrying, would have committed adultery. God cannot just alter the regulations: he must be 'true to his own rules'. So 'Christ meant not to be tak'n word for word'. He was really being ironic: paying the Pharisees out for their trick. 'You' meant not Jews in general, but 'licentious men of your sort'. Christ was saying: 'In so far as Moses' ruling affects your type of man, it is a reflection on your hardheartedness'. As for the second half of his reply, 'from the beginning' shows that he was thinking about what it was like in Eden before the fall. So his equation of remarriage with adultery does not apply to our world at all: it is a description of what would be true if man had not fallen: a piece of irrelevant idealism.

If Milton appears to be standing on his head in this exposition, it is because the words will only suit his purposes that way up. From the time of the divorce tracts on, the term 'nature' plays an increasing part in his arguments. It is 'against nature' to make incompatible people cohabit: so if the Bible does not say they may separate, it must be forced to. He appeals against all law to 'the blameles nature of man', 'the guiltles instinct of nature'. If another writer used these phrases we might suppose that he had a high opinion of human nature in general. With Milton, we know the contrary is true. In the same pamphlet (*The Doctrine and Discipline of Divorce*, 1643), for instance, he can be found gloomily seconding *Genesis* viii, 21 on the inevitable wickedness of the human heart, and rhapsodising about 'the faultless proprieties of nature' which no law, biblical or otherwise, can be permitted to impair. 'Nature', for Milton, is a purely personal convenience: a respectable front for what his own instincts demand. More and more, it becomes the sole criterion: 'I suppose no man of cleare judgement need goe furder to be guided than by the very principles of nature in him' (this is from his argument that it is 'natural' to exterminate Charles I). In *Tetrachordon* (1645) he takes it as axiomatic that 'no ordinance human or from heav'n can binde against the good of man'. It is the voice of Eve, just before she picks the apple: 'Forbids us good, forbids us to be wise?/Such prohibitions bind not' (*PL* ix, 759–60). We see why it has been said that if Milton had been in Adam's place he would have picked the apple at once and written a pamphlet justifying it.

Impatience of restraint reflects in the imagery of Milton's prose. Good is 'lightsome' or fluid: God intended marriage to provide 'free and lightsome conversation'; the body should 'render lightsome, cleare, and not lumpish obedience to the minde'; truth is a fountain, 'if her waters flow not in a perpetuall progression, they sick'n into a muddy pool of conformity'. Congealment is evil: bishops, 'like a seething pot set to coole', settle to 'a skinny congealment of ease and sloth'; Christ's words on divorce must not be 'congeal'd into a stony rigour'; 'acts of worship', when merely repetitive, 'harden into a crust of Formallitie'. Reformation is seen as a 'thaw' melting 'clamm'd' traditions, whereas restrictive legislation and censorship produce as 'stark and dead' a 'congealment' as 'any January could freeze together'.

The images draw on organic processes almost exclusively for the purpose of conveying disgust. There is no complementary strain of healthful bodily functions. The bishops are ulcers, noisome tumours, vomit, gangrene, 'belching the soure crudities of yesterdayes Poperie', emitting a 'loud stench' from feet and mouth. Bishop Hall particularly is endowed with a 'tetter' (skin eruption) and a 'tenasmus' (a continual inclination to void the contents of the bowels, but with little or no discharge, explains the *OED*). He is invited to 'Wipe his fat corpulencies out of our light'. Flesh and related expressions ('slimy fleshlinesse', for example) are terms of abuse, as are the circumstances of birth and generation: Rome, the 'womb' of apostasy; greedy ordinands, 'sordid sperm'; the seditious, 'Abortive Spawne'. The divorce pamphlets have a vested interest in elevating intellectual over bodily intercourse (Milton's confident division of the two itself implies a limit to his human understanding): physical love is reduced to the satisfaction of 'an impetuous nerve', transferring from person to person 'the quintessence of an excrement'. When in the middle of all this we discover Milton blaming the bishops for debarring the common people from the communion table— 'they have made profane that nature which God hath not only cleans'd, but Christ also hath assum'd'—the hypocrisy takes our breath away. Loathing of flesh and plebs is of the very fibre of his writing.

A third type of image (at times connected with the Puritan notion of Rome as Whore of Babylon) arranges women in various degrading postures: 'in a flaring tire bespeckl'd . . . with all the gaudy allurements of a Whore' (this is the Gospel, when the bishops have finished with it); episcopacy has 'pluckt the gay feathers of her obsolet bravery to hide her own deformed barenesse'. The savage eroticism resident in such images becomes patent when, for example, Milton threatens to 'unpinne' Bishop Hall's 'spruce fastidious oratory, to rumple her laces, her frizzles, and her bobins, though she wince, and fling, never so Peevishly'. Although willing to indulge himself in this kind of imagining, Milton is chastely horrified whenever any opponent supposes him to have sexual experience. The suggestion that he visits brothels is met in the *Apology* (1642) with an indignant excursus on his clean living: he justifies his 'obscene' style in controversy by hunting out dirty words in the Bible. Meanwhile he plainly feels that any mention of his enemies' sex-life will help to disgrace them, and collects the scraps industriously. The allegedly henpecked Salmasius becomes 'a foul Circean beast, a filthy pig well used to serving a woman in the lowest sort of slavery'. Charles I 'even in the theatre . . . kisses women wantonly, enfolds their waists and, to mention no more openly, plays with the breasts of maids and mothers'. Both these excerpts are from the *Defence of the English People* (1651) and give a fair indication of its level. Among his charges against the bishops is that they encouraged 'mixt dancing'—'a horror to think'.

It may be retorted that the whole climate of controversy in Milton's day was scabrous: that (however awkward one may feel being reduced to such a plea) he was no worse than others. The point of our inspection is not censure, though—merely the detection of the individual lines Milton's images follow. The notorious 'scurrility' amounts, besides, to something of inestimably greater value than the 'noble' passages, since it exerts Milton's verbal creativity and shows him tapping seams of the language which his poetry passes over. He inflates his enemies into grotesques who lurch or swagger around their ringmaster: a prelate with his 'many-benefice-gaping mouth . . . his canary-sucking, and swan-eating palat'; ecclesiastical dignitaries 'under Sayl in all their Lawn, and Sarcenet, their shrouds, and tackle' and mitres ('the stampe of his cloven foot whom they serve'), descending to 'a Surplice Brabble, a Tippet-scuffle'; a scholar 'wading to his auditors up to the eyebrows in deep shallows that wet not the instep'. In their 'gaudy rottennesse', caked with 'vitious and harden'd excrements', these richly sensuous creatures are usually imprisoned in Milton's imagination by the constraints of epic dignity. Here they rise into the daylight, splendidly bespattered, and parade their loathsomeness. The freak-show is constantly straying into the menagerie. The exhibits become wolves or lions or geese or caterpillars, 'dorrs and horsflies', 'bauling whippets and shin-barkers'. 'The obscene, and surfeited Priest scruples not to paw, and mammock the sacramentall bread as familiarly as his Tavern Bisket.' Milton, whatever he may think, is no longer writing religious controversy. We are in the shadow-land of surpliced apes, monsters in taverns, the kaleidoscopic world that Comus shakes about.

Because Milton's pamphlets exude pride and egotism, their healthy side is often underestimated. That men who are supposed to represent Christ should imitate him in unworldliness and poverty; that they should not be in alliance with any state or government, since he was not; that couples who hate each other should not live together; that people have a right to rise against a tyrannical regime; that it is foolish to allocate power according to the chance of birth: these are his propositions, and they command assent irrespective of what we feel about his personality. If we admire these progressive elements in Milton's thought we are likely to be attracted by the vehemence with which he urges their implementation. Particularly refreshing are his rejoinders to the familiar complacencies about not setting the world right in a day: 'We must not run they say into sudden extreams. This is a fallacious Rule'; 'They say...the government of Episcopacy is now . . . weav'd into the common Law. In God's name let it weave out again.'

It is difficult to feel satisfied with the kind of victory which God and His Son win in *Paradise Lost*, and since Milton's prose is unequivocally derisive of the intervention of force in spiritual affairs, a reading of it aggravates the difficulty. 'God', he advises the prelates in *The Reason of Church-Government* (1642):

> measures . . . strength by suffering, dignity by lowlinesse. . . .When he meant to subdue the world and hell at once . . . it had bin a small maistery for him to have drawn out his Legions into array, and flankt them with his thunder; therefore he sent Foolishness to confute Wisdom, Weakness to bind Strength, Despisedness to vanquish Pride.                                                      Yale i, 824

The Christian God, yes: but not the God of *Paradise Lost*. On the other hand, in Milton's support of the naked assertion of force by the army in 1648-9 the lineaments of his epic-God are easily discernible. So, too, in the hysterical revenge-fantasy which rounds off his first brush with the bishops:

they . . . , after a shamefull end in this Life (which God grant them) shall be throwne downe eternally into the darkest and deepest Gulfe of Hell, where under the despightfull controule, the trample and spurne of all the other Damned, that in the anguish of their Torture shall have no other ease then to exercise a Raving and Bestiall Tyranny over them as their Slaves and Negroes, they shall remaine in that plight for ever, the basest, the lowermost, the most dejected, most underfoot and downe-trodden Vassals of Perdition.

OF REFORMATION, Yale i, 616–17

Milton, in *Colasterion*, feels sure that Christ was merely exaggerating when he recommended turning the other cheek (*Matthew* v, 39–40).

## THE SONNETS

The sonnets composed in these prose years also suffer from double-talk about violence. 'What can War but endless war still breed?' asks the sonnet to Fairfax (XV), yet Cromwell is applauded in his sonnet (XVI) for ploughing his way to peace via 'Darwen stream with blood of Scots imbru'd'. Milton moves around the problem indecisively: Cromwell is reminded that 'peace hath her victories/No less renown'd than war'; Fairfax must rescue 'Truth and Right' from 'Violence'; Sir Henry Vane (XVII) is told that the Roman senate defeated Pyrrhus and Hannibal with 'gowns not arms'—only in a manner of speaking, of course, and religion, it is made clear, 'leans/In peace' on Vane's 'firm hand' because she knows that it can be effectively warlike. 'Avenge, O Lord, thy slaughter'd Saints' (XVIII) leaves the fighting to God, and hopes that the persecuted Protestants can run away in time—'Early may fly the Babylonian woe'. In fact they won a decisive victory over the Catholic troops the same year (1655).

This sonnet is journalistic in its detail: the mother and infant rolled down the rocks, the alpine cold, come fresh from accounts of the massacre. Cromwell's agent, Sir Samuel Morland, reported that the wife of one villager, Giovanni Parise, was hurled down a precipice by the Piedmontese soldiers with her baby in her arms: the baby survived. Many villagers tried to escape into France by the St. Julian pass, and died in the snow. Milton, as Secretary, had spent 25 May 1655 dictating letters of protest from Cromwell to the European heads-of-state. The sonnet emerges directly from this experience, and of all the sonnets it is the only one that manages to be unswervingly topical and great. The others either clutter themselves with dead wood of the 'Worcester's laureate wreath' kind, and sink (this goes for the Cromwell, Vane and Fairfax sonnets), or shake off their topical jackets, and float.

> And the repeated air
> Of sad Electra's poet had the pow'r
> To save the Athenian Walls from ruin bare.
>
> VIII

This has magnificently little to do with the Royalist advance on London after Edgehill. Similarly Isocrates and 'that dishonest victory/At Chaeronea, fatal to liberty' which 'Kill'd with report that Old man eloquent' (X) have wisely lost sight of Lady Margaret Ley and her father. Even 'Methought I saw my late espoused Saint' (XXIII) is greater because we can feel that it speaks for all vanishing dreams, all lost beauty. (Scholarly tussles about *which* wife Milton was dreaming of revealingly seem beside the point.) Of the two sonnets on his blindness we remember one and forget the other because one leaves Milton behind and ends up among the four highest orders of angels who 'stand and wait' around God's throne, while the other lands us on earth beside the *Defence of the English People* ('my noble task').

Of course Milton's effort to climb through his fourteen lines on to the level of the great eternals does not always come off. He may finish solemnly stranded on a heap of platitudes (he does in 'Lady that in the prime', IX, and 'When Faith and Love', XIV). But the effort itself is unmistakable. Time and its passage are used particularly frequently as a way out of the sonnet's immediate locality. This had happened in the earliest sonnet 'O Nightingale' ('Now timely sing . . . As thou from year to year hast sung too late'), and provides the theme of 'How soon hath Time' (VII). 'Though later born than to have known the days . . .'

(X), 'When thou taught'st Cambridge and King Edward Greek' (XI), 'Time will run/On smoother till Favonius re-inspire/The frozen earth' (XX), 'For other things mild Heav'n a time ordains' (XXI), are other attempts, more or less successful, to open up time-perspectives behind or in front of their poems. No doubt the obsession with time and history goes deeper, and reflects Milton's anxiety in these years. 'When I consider how my light is spent,/Ere half my days'. Life less than half over at forty-four? Milton had to give himself time: his great poem was not yet written.

# 7

## *Paradise Lost*: The Objectionable Epic

*Paradise Lost* is great because it is objectionable. It spurs us to
protest. Hence its continued life, when epic genre and heroic
mood are dead. No doubt Milton could have written a poem in
which Satan was utterly evil, Adam obviously wrong. In fact
there were theological reasons against it. A black Satan would
raise the question of how God had created him and would,
besides, remove the possibility of temptation (Milton thought
Spenser a good teaching poet because he had made evil look
good). Also, if the devils were rotten right through bad men
could feel superior to them (ii, 482–5). With a bungling Adam we
could reasonably ask why God had placed our destinies in such
hands. We should curse our 'frail Original' (ii, 374–5), as Satan
hopes we will. If any fallen man reading the poem felt convinced
he would have done better than Adam, Milton would have
failed, and God have picked an unrepresentative representative.

Maybe, but, it will be asked, why is there so little to choose
between Milton's God and his Satan? Surely God should look
more attractive? One answer is that God and Satan dramatise
two powerful elements in Milton's own character—authoritar-
ianism and rebelliousness—so in-fighting is what we should
expect. But also, there is no need to assume that Milton found
God's ways, in the Bible, 'attractive'. That was beside the point.
Theology was a science, not an art, and he was out to discover
the truth about God, pleasant or otherwise. That God did punish
innocent children for their parents' sins, he was sure, and he
illustrates the practice, in *Christian Doctrine*, by alluding to the
treatment women and children receive at the hands of conquering
armies. We are not to imagine that he thought conquering armies

pleasant, only that he knew them to be factual. Most men, he believed, were going to find God's ways unattractive in the last resort. It is not always noticed that Milton does not say he is going to 'justify the ways of God to men' (i, 26), but admits he needs help to do it. Moreover 'justify' could mean not 'make excuses for' but 'demonstrate' or 'prove'—more like 'assert', in the line before. That, for his own part, he found the classical myths more beautiful than the Christian is clearly indicated by the astonishing poetry he writes when he is able to get back to them in *Paradise Lost* (e.g. i, 738–46; iv, 268–72; vii, 32–9. There are no 'Christian' moments to match these poetically). But beauty, he knew, was not truth. When God turns Adam and Eve out of the garden, Milton does not shrink from figuring their expulsion in brutal ikons of swooping eagle and preying lion (xi, 185–90).

GOD

Milton first intended to write *Paradise Lost* as a drama. The drafts he has left show that it would have meant leaving out all the dramatic elements. Adam and Eve could not have come on stage until everything was over and they were decently covered, and the bravado of putting God into the witness-box would have been impossible.

The theoretical attributes of Milton's God are impressive: he is 'Omnipotent,/Immutable, Immortal, Infinite' (iii, 372–3), 'All-seeing', 'Omniscient' and 'in all things wise and just' (x, 6–7). We are not meant to take these seriously (we are not meant, for instance, to point out that an immutable being cannot know what it is like to change, but that an omniscient one must). We are supposed to accept them unquestioningly. Most readers do, and are not worried by the impossibility of God's attributes but by his failure to live up to them. The Old Testament, it is fair to say, might worry them equally. To modern eyes the God found there is a praise-hungry, vindictive racialist who punishes ceremonial irregularities with death and showers his enemies with fire and brimstone (*Psalms* xi, 6). Milton's is not an unflattering portrait.

76

More particularly the *Genesis* creation-and-fall story has two Gods because it had two authors. The so-called Priestly writer, responsible for i, 1–ii, 4, posited an abstract, elevated God who creates man in his image. The Jahwist, responsible for the rest of the *Genesis* account, had in mind a cruder sort of God who makes man out of dust and is anxious about magic trees. The myth the Jahwist was purveying had no high moral import but was meant to explain why we wear clothes and hate snakes. In papering over the cracks between the two Gods Milton had centuries of Christian exegesis to help him, and that we can still sense their distinct presences in his poem is a testimony to the honesty with which he has here read the Bible.

The Bible says that God's laughter is scornful and derisive (*Psalms* ii, 4). Some readers feel that Milton has filled this out a little too enthusiastically. God's humour comes near to misrepresentation, as when he pretends that Satan has escaped Hell because it was unable to hold him (iii, 84), though really he let him out himself (i, 210–13), or as when he makes out that he is not omnipotent. This second joke unfortunately involves the Son who, though he does not laugh (his face remains 'serene'), congratulates his father on his witticism and himself on the glory he will gain at the expense of his erring brothers (v, 733–42). God's banter with Adam about why he should want a woman (viii, 368–451) is less amiable if you recall that the one he intends to supply will, he knows, be the death of Adam. Besides, for God to mislead Adam, in this scene, about his real purposes marriagewise merely 'for trial' (viii, 447) appears irresponsible. Might not Adam think the tree-prohibition merely for trial too, as Satan suggests it is (ix, 692–7)?

It is not only when God is joking that he seems to put things in a false light. We can accept that he sends angels on needless errands (viii, 238–40), because an omnipotent God who, on biblical evidence, sends angels on errands, must do so needlessly. But when Milton's God tells Michael to 'drive out' the rebels, he gives an order which he knows Michael cannot perform (vi, 52, 702–3), and has indeed taken care to furnish only half the available forces (vi, 49, compare ii, 692). God's assurance at the end of the second day's battle that sin has not sensibly impaired the bad angels ('for I suspend thir doom'), does not accord with the facts (see vi, 401–5, 661). It is hard to take him seriously, too, when he announces, after the bad angels have been thrown out, that mankind, 'by degrees of merit rais'd', will repopulate Heaven. He can foresee the fall, and after that there will be no question of man getting to Heaven by 'merit'. God's explanation of why man has to be expelled from Paradise also arouses our suspicions. From what he says to the Son he seems to put it down to a sort of chemical reaction, beyond his control—the 'pure immortal Elements' of the garden 'Eject' Adam of their own accord, because he is 'tainted' (xi, 50–3). This, however, would dispense with the need to expel him, and besides, Paradise does not remain 'pure', it is parched (xii, 636) by the avenging angels, and ends up as 'an Island salt and bare' (xi, 834). A few moments later God gives the angels a quite different reason for turning man out, that otherwise man might eat from the tree of life and live for ever; but his jocular hint that immortality is not so easy to get ('dream at least to live/For ever') makes this reason self-defeating as well (xi, 93–6). When he advises Michael to select particularly fiery warriors for the job, in case Satan should interfere, he must know Satan will not. The angelic nuclear explosion which he plans (xii, 629–36) must be simply to intimidate two refugees.

The arguments with which Milton supplies God are dramatically invigorating precisely because they spark off so many objections. Adam, he says, 'had of mee/All he could have' (iii, 97–8). This cannot mean 'all I could give him', since omnipotence is talking. It apparently means 'all he could have, without becoming something other than man'. But that makes God's claim circular, because he fixed the limits of manhood in the first place. It is not to be suspected that God could not have made Adam so that he would not fall. He explains that he stood to get more pleasure from the obedience of a fallible Adam, which is why he made him like that (iii, 107); but the motive has a limited appeal even, one would have thought, to God, who knew beforehand that the pleasure would never materialise. 'Die hee or Justice must' (iii, 210) strikes weakly. Since God foresaw the whole affair it is, we feel, late for him to be invoking principles. He should have found a way out. Of course, he has: the death of his Son, but that solution has a doubtful effect on us when Father and Son are separate beings. When they are one, as in the standard theology, God offers himself. But Milton proved that they were distinct in *Christian Doctrine*, and presents each free-standing in his poem. Consequently God seems apart from the crucifixion. And we are disappointed to find that 'He with his whole posterity must die' (iii, 209) is a mere tantrum, with no force of necessity behind it, because some of Adam's posterity do not die (xi, 709). More important, this plain warning about Adam's posterity is never given to the person it most concerns, Adam. Milton was here in difficulties with the *Genesis* account. It does not say that Adam and Eve were ever immortal, or that their sin passed to their descendants (these were later Christian refinements), so there is no question of Adam being warned about his children. God simply tells him he will die the day he eats the apple, and he does not. Milton sidles round this by making his God say what the Bible says: 'The day thou eat'st thereof . . . thou shalt die' (viii, 329–30), and immediately offer an alternative forecast: 'From that day mortal, and this happy State/Shalt lose' (331–2). That, anyway, is how Adam recollects it, though in Raphael's version there is just the misleading notice of instant death given in the Bible—'in the day thou eat'st, thou di'st' (vii, 544)—and Milton later talks of 'th'instant stroke of Death denounc't that day' being 'Remov'd far off' (x, 210–11), as if Raphael's were the more accurate account of what God had said. Of course, he knew it was, since he had made the other one up himself. Milton plainly realised that Adam could not, from the Bible account alone, be warned about his children or blamed for their death, because the *Genesis* Adam had God's word for it, when he ate the apple, that he would not survive to have any. The poem's Adam says he had no expectation of surviving to become a father (x, 1048–50). In this matter, then, Milton's attempt to keep in line with theological tradition but be faithful to *Genesis* as well has produced a God who seems to hush up the (from our viewpoint) worst result of the fall until afterwards. It may be added that Adam's 'Did I request thee, Maker, from my Clay/To mould me Man?' (x, 743-4) is a most telling question. The exoneration of God that Milton promptly whips up— 'then should have been refus'd/Those terms whatever, when they were propos'd'—does not make sense in the circumstances, since by the time any terms could be proposed Adam had already been created. The answer does not satisfy even Adam for long, and he is again complaining about life being 'Obtruded' on mankind at xi, 502-7.

God gets caught between *Genesis* and the theologians again over the serpent's punishment. In *Genesis* the serpent is the tempter—no Satan appears. But once the story is sophisticated and the serpent becomes nothing but an overcoat, punishing it seems mere spite. Milton is reduced to muddle. He says that the snake was just an instrument, but it was nevertheless right to punish it, though the punishment really landed on Satan, yet crippled the snake as well (x, 165-77; ix, 496-7). God moves, we know, in a mysterious way, but this seems to leave the snake with room for complaint. If its nature really was 'vitiated' (spoiled) by what had happened, as Milton vaguely suggests (perhaps having a demon inside it overtaxed its strength, so it could never go upright again), then there was no need to curse it anyway.

We have a nagging suspicion, too, that the treatment of the fallen angels does not fit very brightly into God's plan. Origen (A.D. 185-254), the great Alexandrian theologian, some of whose ideas Milton shared, thought that the devils would eventually be forgiven. Milton's God says unequivocally that they will not, and the Son does not put in a word for them, though he reflects his Father's love which is theoretically 'without end' (iii, 142). God justifies his tough line with the argument that the rebel angels fell 'by thir own suggestion' (iii, 129), not misled by Satan, whereas man fell 'deceiv'd' (130). Raphael tells Adam, though, that Satan 'infus'd/Bad influence into th'unwary breast/Of his Associate' (v, 695-6). It is not merely sentimental to bother about the devils. The Son asks God, discussing Adam's fall, 'Shall the Adversary thus obtain/His end, and frustrate thine?' (iii, 156-7)—

expecting the answer no. But does not Satan frustrate God's end by being so wicked that he can never be saved? Or was the eternal torment of a third of his angels always part of God's design? By God's account, all his works are dear to him (iii, 277), which must include Satan. One way of clearing God is generously hit on by Satan himself (iv, 100-4): if Satan were forgiven he would only fall again and have to be punished even harder. Yet when we reflect that God knew all this before he made Satan, and chose to make him, the excuse pales.

The devils' case is interesting because it is much the same as our own. The doctrine of the 'fortunate fall'—God's production of 'all this good' out of 'evil', as Adam puts it (xii, 470)—boils down to an omnipotent and omniscient figure getting round the picking of an apple (an act of no intrinsic significance) at the expense of the suffering and death of all, and the everlasting torment of the 'far greater part' (xii, 533), of mankind. Adam's elation over the wonderful cleverness of this plan only makes us feel that he has had all the stuffing knocked out of him by God's tricks.

God's exaltation of the Son (v, 600-15), which starts all the trouble, is deliberately doctored by Milton so that it sounds provocative compared with its source (*Hebrews* i, 6). It seems to have been his own idea to make this exaltation the factor that pushes Satan across the heavenly Rubicon. Lactantius had traced Satan's rebellion to envy of the Son (others had put it down to resentment over the creation of men or disgust at the news that Christ was to become one). Milton's Satan hits on the idea that the promotion of the Son is unfair. God, we cannot help feeling, needlessly gives some colour to the charge by using the word 'begot' in the text of his announcement when he means 'promoted'. The natural inference is that it is a new arrival being up-graded. There is no apparent need for adoration of the Son to be commanded so peremptorily. If the Son deserves it—and God rests his case on 'merit' (vi, 43)—then presumably, given a heavenly ambience, the adoration will follow uncommanded, unless the merit is apparent only to God. God's challenging tone makes it sound as if he anticipates rebellion (which, of course, he does). We suspect he has noticed there are some sub-standard angels about (Mammon, unable to take his eyes off the golden pavement, and so on) and needs a pretext to throw them out. Though his decrees are theoretically irrevocable and eternal, he appears to feel that he should issue this one a second time. The proclamation in Book v is not exactly duplicated by the later one (iii, 317–18), but reading the two we find that God sets the Son over the angels twice.

God prods the devils into rebellion, then. He also exposes man to a temptation to which he knows he will succumb. The effect of God's exhibition with the scales, as has been noted, is to let Satan get away when he is faced with inevitable defeat (iv, 995–7). When his elaborately redundant police force makes its one arrest God realises the prisoner is a homicidal maniac and lets him go at once. This twisted behaviour is matched when God looks down on Adam and Eve 'with pity' (v, 220) and immediately takes steps to make their fall more heinous (render them 'inexcusable', as the *Argument* to Book v puts it) by sending a warning which he knows will be ignored.

Vindictiveness, anger, and a passion for self-aggrandisement are three characteristics that bind Milton's God to his Satan. Heaven's morality is one of vengeance (iii, 399) as well as Hell's. Milton had plenty of biblical authority for making God vengeful (e.g. *Deuteronomy* xxxii, 35). His God, though, seems less perceptive than Satan, in that Satan becomes sufficiently adult to see through revenge: 'Revenge, at first though sweet,/Bitter ere long back on itself recoils' (ix, 171–2). When Adam turns vengeful after the fall he knows he is following God's example (x, 1023–36). As for anger, God realises himself that he has a reputation for irascibility (x, 626–7), but talks about his anger as if it were beyond his control (iii, 187, 275). Even the Son seems to think there is no chance of calming it, only of putting oneself in its way (iii, 237). Gabriel is of the opinion that it is 'infinite' (iv, 916), and Raphael believes that if God had been interrupted while at work on the world, he might have flown into a rage and smashed it up (viii, 234–6). A God who frequently gets into such a state that he gives off smoke and flame (ii,

263–8; vi, 56–9) is hard put to it to look decent in a poem that places such emphasis upon the control of passion by reason. The anger is biblical, but Milton puts God's anger beside the Greek ethic. Similarly the poem is quietly scornful of those who value 'the praise of men' (iii, 453), but exhibits a God whose main thought is about his own glory (iii, 133). The Son recognises that this was the whole motive for the creation (iii, 164). We are struck by the note of self-advertisement in God's voice, even when he is being merciful: 'Man shall not quite be lost, but sav'd who will,/Yet not of will in him, but grace in me' (iii, 173–4).

Uncomfortableness about Milton's God, plus the realisation that he can produce scriptural credentials, are indispensable sources of the poem's force. It grips because he is morally repellent but theoretically unfaultable. Shelley, in the *Defence of Poetry*, remarks:

> Milton has so far violated the popular creed . . . as to have alleged no superiority of moral virtue to his God over his Devil. And this bold neglect of a direct moral purpose is the most decisive proof of Milton's genius.

The irascible eccentric on the mountain top shoots turbulent energies through the whole narrative frame which an 'acceptable' figure could never have radiated. To have made God 'mysterious and vague', as C. S. Lewis would like, so that he should 'escape criticism', would be to prune the work of half its knotty power. Milton did not really believe in the God of the Bible, so there was always, as it were, an escape clause. God, he explained in *Christian Doctrine*, is far beyond man's thoughts, and the Bible accounts, both literal and figurative, are adaptations made to fit the crudity of our understanding. But, on the other hand, God has chosen this way of revealing himself to us, and Milton was insistent that we must not flinch from taking what he says literally:

> Why should we hesitate to believe about God what God himself has not hesitated to say clearly about himself? . . . If after six days' work God is said to be 'refreshed by rest', *Exod.* xxxi, 17, or if he is said to 'fear the wrath of the enemy', *Deut.* xxxii, 27, let us not think it

beneath God to be refreshed by what refreshed him or to fear what he feared. For however much you may try to soften down these and similar recorded facts about God with long and roundabout interpretations, it comes to the same thing in the end.

CHRISTIAN DOCTRINE I, ii, Columbia xiv, 34–6

It is with this shattering frankness that God's part in *Paradise Lost* is written.

## GOOD ANGELS

Since the good angels are ultimately useless, and know it (viii, 237–40), they provide a ponderous by-play to the main affairs of the poem. Apparently it takes a good angel to recognise his own inutility. At any rate, when Belial is speaking in Hell, his assumption that God needs to send patrols into no-man's-land to forestall surprise attacks passes without comment (ii, 132–4). Belial knows, when he thinks about it, that God 'Views all things at one view' (ii, 188–90), but fails to put two and two together. Raphael does so, and does not mind that the answer makes him redundant. The choice in Heaven lies between imperceptiveness and flunkeyism. It does not leave Raphael in a good position to lecture Adam about 'self-esteem' (viii, 572).

The good angels suffer 'rage' like the bad ones (vi, 635), and their sense of humour is as cruel and childish. It would take a nice ear to distinguish the 'great laughter' (xii, 52–62) in Heaven which follows God's practical joke at Babel from Satan's merriment over the effects of his cannon. Uriel is distinctly cool about angels who do not bother to come and look at God's new toy —'what some perhaps/Contented with report, hear only in Heav'n' (iii, 700–1). Add to this Gabriel's unwholesome jibes about Satan fawning and cringing in front of God's throne (iv, 959), and the gladness of Raphael and his colleagues on hearing such ghastly noises coming out of Hell (viii, 244–5), and the society in Heaven does not seem to have been ideal either before the fall of the angels or after it.

Interestingly Michael does not appear to have noticed Satan's creepy side, since he thought that all was well in Heaven (vi, 262–3). This suggests that he is either less sharp or less spiteful than Gabriel. It is strange to hear Michael so strong against violence (xi, 428) when we last saw him chopping down 'Squadrons at once' with a two-handed sword (vi, 251). When Michael informs Adam that people would not get diseases if they stuck to 'The rule of not too much' (xi, 515–37), he strikes us as scandalously misinformed (and must have struck Milton so, too: compare *Samson Agonistes* 698–702). Indeed the poet's question, as Michael and Adam stand watching the hospital-cases, 'Sight so deform what heart of Rock could long/Dry-ey'd behold?', and its answer, 'Adam could not', implies that there is something shamefully unfeeling about Michael (xi, 494–5).

When Uriel slides down a sunbeam to get to the earth, it seems an ingenious way to travel, though the effect is a little spoiled when we see that one has to hang about until sundown for the return trip (iv, 589–92). However, we are disappointed with Uriel when he fails to pierce Satan's disguise, especially as the excuse Milton offers ('neither Man nor Angel can discern/Hypocrisy . . . Invisible, except to God alone' iii, 682–4) turns out to be less than half true. Angels, we find, are equipped with infallible disguise-piercers (iv, 811–12), so it seems careless of Uriel not to have used his, and Sin and Death can tell Satan at a glance 'though in disguise' (x, 331). It is unbecoming for 'The sharpest-sighted Spirit of all in Heav'n' (iii, 690–1) to have to confess he lost sight of Satan in some shadows (iv, 572–3).

Raphael's warning to Adam is teasingly inadequate. Milton's 'O for that warning voice, which he who saw/Th'Apocalypse, heard cry in Heav'n aloud' (iv, 1–2) itself suggests that something better might have been done. What is more disquieting is that Raphael uses language which could, some readers feel, predispose Eve to fall. He foretells that from 'corporal nutriments' the human pair may 'wingd ascend/Ethereal, as wee' (v, 496–9), and this chimes disastrously with her dream-tempter's information that eating the apple will leave her 'not to earth confin'd,/But sometimes in the Air, as wee' (v, 78–9). Raphael does not, as he might helpfully have done, identify the dream-tempter with Satan, and his choice of simile, 'But Knowledge is as food' (vii, 126), is not tactful in the circumstances. When he boasts to

Adam that he is going to unfold secrets 'perhaps/Not lawful to reveal' (v, 569-70), he is hardly assisting the human pair to take divine prohibitions about knowledge very seriously. He heavily underlines the inferiority of their understanding of the universe to his own, and tantalises them with alternative theories (viii, 122-6), only to condemn the curiosity he has been arousing. Milton's interested account of Galileo and the telescope (i, 287-91) makes us feel that we have him on our side in disbelieving Raphael's assurance that astronomers will never find out whether the earth goes round the sun. Raphael, of course, who must have been present at the assembly in Heaven, has heard it announced that Adam and Eve are to fall. This puts him in an unenviable position from the start, and he cannot be blamed if it seems to involve some duplicity. But when he makes off, with his 'Be strong, live happy, and love' (viii, 633), we wonder whether many visitors to a condemned cell leave so cheerfully. Whereas it is supposed to be both evil and foolish of Satan to deny he was created, Raphael is not eager to count angels as 'creatures' when he tells Adam that man was made 'not prone/And Brute as other Creatures' (vii, 506-7). Nothing more than a significant slip of the tongue, perhaps, but it seems to muddle Adam a little, who, after his conversation with Raphael, can be found talking about men as God's 'prime Creatures' (ix, 940), though he should know, from what Raphael reported of Abdiel's speech, that they are probably not. Another unaccountable thing about Raphael is why he should disguise himself as a phoenix when flying (v, 271-7). He would, surely, be faster with his normal six wings. Possibly he thought it a beautiful idea, like Uriel's sunbeam. If so, it is to his credit.

Even Abdiel's behaviour is directed by self-interest. In Satan's camp he is well aware that he is on a sinking ship, and has little faith in God's discrimination relative to survivors, which is why he gets off so smartly, as he explains (v, 888-92). Returning with legions of angels at his back, he feels he can securely jeer at Satan—'my Sect thou seest' (vi, 147)—and lecture him on political realities—'how vain/Against th'Omnipotent to rise in arms' (135-6). But the argument has no moral weight, and we reflect that if Abdiel were a little less complacent it would occur to him that it is equally vain to rise in arms on behalf of omnipotence.

The remarkable silence of the good angels when God asks for a volunteer to die for man (iii, 217–21) is, Mr. Burden tells us, 'of course no criticism of their virtue', but he then quotes a passage from *Christian Doctrine* which confirms our impression that they lack courage Their fright functions, of course, as contrast, throwing Christ's offer into splendid relief, but it cannot help back-firing on them, especially as Milton has planned that it should associate them with the lesser devils (ii, 417–23), and on God, who is shown, extra-biblically, making an exhibition of his followers for his Son's benefit. Mr Burden means that he does not believe it is meant to be a criticism of their virtue, but he is occupied with a tidier poem which he feels Milton wanted to write.

The armour which the angels wear in the war in Heaven has often been criticised. C. S. Lewis, though, defends it: 'They can be damaged and hurt. A casing of some suitable inorganic material would therefore be a real protection'. It appears from the text that the good angels differ from the bad in being 'Invulnerable' and 'unobnoxious to be pain'd' (vi, 400–4). Even when they are toppled like ninepins, only their pride suffers (vi, 595–607). Armour, strictly, makes the good angels ridiculous, but not the bad.

### THE SON

As in *Christian Doctrine*, Milton makes it heretically plain in the poem that the Son is a separate and subordinate being who owes his exaltation and power to the Father. Even his vice-regency is only temporary (iii, 339–41). These conclusions, Milton believed, were inescapable from a close reading of the Bible. If he had not taken the bold step of building his poem around an irate tyrant, then having to present the Son as a separate person from God might have made him seem inferior. As it is it plays straight into his hands. He is able to make the Son sound as if he is having to deal tactfully with a parent of uncertain temper. 'O Father, gracious was that word which clos'd/Thy sovran sentence' (iii, 144–5) needs only a fractional stress on 'clos'd' to turn it into a reproach; and 'that be from thee far,/That far be from thee, Father' (iii, 153–4) has a fatally coaxing ring. He understands his Father's tastes only too well: 'Thou at the sight/Pleas'd, out of Heaven shalt look down and smile,/While by thee rais'd I ruin all my Foes' (iii, 257–8).

True, the excuse that the Son is merely carrying out the Father's orders, though welcome, does not let us feel entirely comfortable with his bellicose chariot-ride. It is not as if one has to import an alien pacifism into the poem to see the drawbacks of this type of victory. Michael supplies the moral viewpoint when he speaks scathingly of those who think it glorious 'To overcome in battle' (xi, 689–97). It is difficult to deny that this is how the Son thinks: 'Matter to mee of Glory, whom thir hate/Illustrates, when they see all Regal Power/Giv'n me to quell thir pride' (v, 738–40). But at least he feels the need to excuse himself for using such methods (force—he says, in effect—is the only argument they understand, vi, 820–2), and having shot the devils full of arrows and driven over their heads he treats them quite gently: 'The overthrown he rais'd, and as a Herd/Of Goats or timorous flock together throng'd/Drove them before him' (vi, 856–7). Commentators tell us that we should be reminded of the separation of sheep from goats at the last judgment, and Arnold Stein thinks Milton meant to leave the rebels 'exposed to laughter'. Presumably it depends whether you are the sort of person who laughs when sheep and goats are driven over a cliff, but it seems odd behaviour for a Good Shepherd.

The vengeful rationale of the poem stains even its account of the crucifixion, and this, if *Paradise Lost* has a major blemish, must surely be it. Granted, Michael must see things from an angelic viewpoint, but his version is horribly unlike the gospel accounts. 'Father, forgive them; for they know not what they do' are words which *Paradise Lost* cannot include, and the omission is a measure of its spiritual smallness. When Michael puts the hammer into Christ's hands—'But to the Cross he nails thy Enemies' (xii, 415)—we recoil as from an obscenity. (*Colossians* ii, 14, where Christ nails 'the handwriting of ordinances that

was against us . . . to his cross', might be pleaded in mitigation
but it is not a precedent for the image of Christ as executioner.)

## SATAN AND HELL

The best modern commentary on Milton's Satan is David
Halliwell's *Little Malcolm and His Struggle Against the Eunuchs*.
Like Halliwell's Scrawdyke, Satan is a paranoiac. He is obsessed
with his own importance. He cannot reciprocate positive
emotions, and needs to believe that he is persecuted. He chooses
to live in a world of fantasy in which he can make himself
supreme. Because we are individuals, this is a state which lurks
on the threshold of realisation in each of us. In Satan we see it
acted out. That is why we cannot tear ourselves from the
spectacle of his struggle. His states of mind are so familiar to us
that we instinctively excuse them even while our moral self
classifies them as 'wrong'. When he complains of 'The debt
immense of endless gratitude' (iv, 52), we are dishonest if we
pretend that we do not know what he means. The differences
between Satan and Scrawdyke are that Satan's delusions of
grandeur are not entirely delusions—we do not need to be
admirers of 'leadership' to feel the magnetism of Satan's sheer
courage—and he really is persecuted. 'The character of Satan',
wrote Shelley, 'engenders in the mind a pernicious casuistry
which leads us to weigh his faults with his wrongs, and to excuse
the former because the latter exceed all measure'. Moreover, if
we listen for a reverberation of:

> who shall tempt with wand'ring feet
> The dark unbottom'd infinite Abyss
> And through the palpable obscure find out
> His uncouth way, or spread his aery flight
> Upborne with indefatigable wings
> Over the vast abrupt

ii, 404–9

we shall find it coming from Milton himself:

> my advent'rous Song,
> That with no middle flight intends to soar

89

> Above th'Aonian Mount, while it pursues
> Things unattempted yet in Prose or Rhyme.

i, 13–16

and the coincidence weakens our resistance to Satan's force.

The images of <u>dynamism and magnitude</u> heaped upon Satan carry far more conviction than those applied to any other character. When he stumbles across the burning marl, leaning on his spear, 'to equal which the tallest Pine/Hewn on Norwegian hills, to be the Mast/Of some great Ammiral, were but a wand' (i, 292–4), the attentive detailing—'Pine', 'Norwegian'—and the four mild syllables at the end which fling what we had been led to believe a comparison into colossal inadequacy, reveal <u>a resourcefulness in the workmanship</u> which seem never to be called upon when a heavenly inmate is described. It is the same when Satan is touched by Ithuriel's spear, and starts up:

> As when a spark
> Lights on a heap of nitrous Powder, laid
> Fit for the Tun some Magazin to store
> Against a rumour'd War, the Smutty grain
> With sudden blaze diffus'd, inflames the Air.

iv, 814–18

The texture of 'Tun' and 'Smutty' is thickly satisfying, and the sound brilliantly managed, with the quick 'az' of 'Magazin' blowing open to the wide 'az' of 'blaze' as the heap explodes. Yet Satan in both scenes is supposed to be coming off worse. If one turns to the nominal victor—the Son in his Father's optic chariot—the unnatural straining is painfully clear. This would not matter—might even be an advantage—if the heavenly figures were recommended for qualities other than power and size, but the poet is plainly anxious to claim these to a greater degree when God and his Son are around—'above all highth', 'Almighty', 'Grasping ten thousand Thunders'. <u>The more superlatives are used, the smaller the pair seem.</u>

Satan's superiority in depth as well as stature is a matter of <u>better writing.</u> Where else are we allowed to see a character in such varied light as when he talks to himself on Niphates (iv,

*[margin note: Satan in the light of good is graspable.]*

90

32-113)? Adam's fall-soliloquy is the only speech one might risk in its company, and putting them side by side we see how smooth and flat Adam's psychology is by comparison. What other character reacts to anything as complexly as Satan to Eve (ix, 455-93)? Disarmed, his hatred draining away as he basks in the sight, then frantically restoking the furnaces of revenge, then calming to assess the situation, congratulate himself, and so, wistfully, stray back—'divinely fair, fit Love for Gods'—even ponder for a moment on how strange goodness is—'Not terrible, though terror be in Love/And beauty'—swaying, until he grabs himself from the brink—'beauty, not approacht by stronger hate,/Hate stronger'. The audience relaxes: a close thing—and it is; we need to take stock of it. Eve's beauty, just for a moment, took the pain out of Hell. The theory that Satan 'degenerates' or is 'degraded' works out only on a superficial level, because the writing of his part goes on being irresistible. It is true that the wolf and thief similes (iv, 183-91) drop suddenly below the rest: an attempt to trivialise which is at once felt to be ill-judged— what he is about is huge by any account. But a simile like that of the vulture (iii, 431-9) is magnificently fitted out for its job, throwing what is spacious but sterile—'barren Plains' travelled by winds—into fusion with the guileful 'cany Waggons' and the revolting, purposeful bird, conveying its dark menace through the 'snowy ridge' it first stands against. Satan can be reckoned on for poetry and drama right to the end. The poem's best joke (it is not saying much) is 'Him by fraud I have seduc'd/From his Creator, and the more to increase/Your wonder, with an Apple' (x, 485-7), not because it is particularly funny in itself but because Milton lets us share the uncontrollable glee with which Satan tells it. And even as he falls, astonished, out of the poem, he is wrapped in great poetry—the masterpiece of verbal plasticity that fills Pandemonium with serpents (x, 510-32).

Satan's crime in the first place was not so much pride as doubt —intellectual, not moral, and so, we feel, less blameworthy. If he had been as sure as Abdiel that God could see and do everything, his conduct would have been suicidal, and far from impelling him pride must then have withheld him from inevitable humiliation. Alternatively one can diagnose his doubt itself as a symptom of megalomania. At all events God deliberately encouraged it, as Satan complains (i, 642), by fielding only half a side for the first three days' battle. Afterwards, in his speech to the troops, Satan pretends it was God's 'utmost power' they fought against (i, 103), to cheer them up. Of course, he realises now that it was not, but we should not infer that he knew all along that God could make a better showing. He uses the term 'Almighty' of God before the battle (v, 868), and this is sometimes dragged up to prove that 'at heart' he knew what was what. But 'Almighty' was just a title for God, not a profession of faith, and even after his fall Satan, in more confident moments, can be found doubting God's right to it—'he Almighty styled' (ix, 137). To take stock of Satan's temperament we must grasp that mood can alter his beliefs. When he gets back into sight of Heaven, its brilliance moves him deeply, and he finds himself believing that its God really was his creator (iv, 43–4). Because he is here talking to himself, it is sometimes alleged that this must represent his 'true' state of knowledge, so when he told Abdiel earlier that angels were 'self-begot', he was wilfully romancing (v, 860). But the poem will not allow such easy conclusions. In a later soliloquy, when Satan begins to feel that revenge is within his reach, he doubts once more whether the the angels are of God's making (ix, 146–7).

Satan's cruelty to Adam and Eve is the biggest embarrassment to his friends. Professor Empson has heroically endeavoured to read 'Hell shall unfold,/To entertain you two, her widest Gates' (iv, 381–3) as a well-meant invitation. Not many readers feel safe leaning over backwards so far, and they need not, to save the speech from being the merely venomous irony that Professor Empson wants to avoid. Satan's previous line, 'Accept your Maker's work: he gave it me' (iv, 380), is true. We call Satan cruel at God's expense. We are acquainted early on with the ingenuity which 'infinite goodness' has expended on making Hell as painful as possible, and even the demons are horrified to discover the ovens and refrigerators waiting for mankind (ii, 596–616—Milton was following a recipe for damned souls in the apocryphal *Book of the Secrets of Enoch* x, 1). Shelley has made the God-Satan parallel look as good for Satan as is possible:

> Implacable hate, patient cunning, and a sleepless refinement of device to inflict the extremest anguish on an enemy, these things are evil; and, although venial in a slave, are not to be forgiven in a tyrant; although redeemed by much that ennobles his defeat in one subdued, are marked by all that dishonours his conquest in the victor. Milton's Devil as a moral being is as far superior to his God, as one who perseveres in some purpose which he has conceived to be excellent in spite of adversity and torture, is to one who in the cold security of undoubted triumph inflicts the most horrible revenge upon his enemy, not from any mistaken notion of inducing him to repent of a perseverance in enmity, but with the alleged design of exasperating him to deserve new torments.
>
> A DEFENCE OF POETRY: WORKS, ed.
> Ingpen and Peck, vii, 129

Shelley's nobility almost persuades us, but its flaw is inescapable. 'To inflict the extremest anguish on an enemy'; we admit, reluctantly, that this has to read 'on an enemy's children', before it will fit Satan. When he broods over Adam and Eve he sees vividly that he is taking revenge on creatures 'who wrong me not'; he feels himself 'Melt' at their innocence (iv, 387–9)— presumably we are to imagine him moved to tears, as he was before his defeated army. Yet he decides to murder innocence. Even if we do not detest him, we are obliged to confess that there is nothing to save him from detestation. Comparisons with God no longer help. Satan's superior stature now tells against him. He looms above the naked figures, adult, aware, but evil: Milton's God, by comparison, is in querulous second childhood. C. S. Lewis, treating the poem as if it took place in North Oxford, says that Satan degenerates into 'a thing that peers in at bedroom or bathroom windows', but besides the fact that such a stone is not safe to throw in a poem which contains an all-seeing God, it minimises a momentous situation. If Satan were out for nothing but a little voyeurism we should be very happy with him. But to imagine him 'writhing in prurience as he overlooks the privacy of two lovers' is to make it sound too enjoyable:

> Sight hateful, sight tormenting! thus these two
> Imparadis't in one another's arms
> The happier Eden, shall enjoy thir fill
> Of bliss on bliss, while I to Hell am thrust.

iv, 505–8

Peeping Toms do not gnash their teeth so.

We are, of course, frequently reminded that Satan is doing his best to imitate God (ii, 511; v, 764, etc.), and he is remarkably successful. The oriental allusions (meant to sound heathenish and degenerate), and warnings like 'barbaric' stuck on to Satan's 'Pearl and Gold' (ii, 4), distinguish his despotism only incidentally from God's. Both are totalitarian. Gold, crowns and thrones are as surely symbols of worth in Heaven as in Pandemonium. Heaven even shared the same architect (i, 732–3). Critics who feel superior to Pandemonium's bad taste would probably go no further into Heaven than the self-operating diamond and gold doors on musical hinges (iii, 506; vii, 206, 566). Both devils and angels exercise their bodies, but only the devils exercise their minds (ii, 528–61; iv, 551–2). 'Pomp' is inexplicably bad in Hell (and on earth), but good in Heaven (ii, 510; v, 354; vii, 564).

This rapport between God and Satan is deepened by the suggestion that it is because Satan finds God so lovable that he has to hate him. Love would threaten his self-sufficiency. We get a hint of this when Satan feels he 'could love' the human pair because 'so lively shines/In them Divine resemblance' (iv, 363–4). God's love for Satan takes the form of hatred, too. Their twisted relationship has a strange closeness which makes that between God and his Son seem formal. We see that there are times when they understand each other perfectly (iv, 98–104). 'For never can true reconcilement grow/Where wounds of deadly hate have pierc'd so deep' might be Samson wavering over Dalila. This inviting aspect of the quarrel in Heaven is not explored far by Milton, but it is drawn in.

Picking holes in the logic of the other devils has provided

critics with an innocent pastime, and they are the one kind of hole everyone agrees Milton 'put there'—Beelzebub saying they have 'endanger'd Heav'n's perpetual King' (i, 131), unaware of the contradiction, and so forth. At this level the debate in Hell is rather mechanically undermined. It gathers life with Belial's 'for who would lose,/Though full of pain, this intellectual being,/Those thoughts that wander through eternity' (ii, 146–8). We are made to feel that Belial has a mind, where the rest have only arguments. But the poem stacks its cards against him. 'Wander' is one of its key verbs, and it belongs to the lost, the fallen: 'Thir wand'ring Gods disguis'd in brutish forms' (i, 481); 'then wander forth the Sons/Of Belial' (i, 501–2); 'And found no end, in wand'ring mazes lost' (ii, 561); and so on, through Satan as a 'wand'ring Fire' (ix, 634) and Eve's 'Desire of wand-'ring this unhappy Morn' (ix, 1136), to 'They hand in hand with wand'ring steps and slow' (xii, 648). Belial's lyricism is booby-trapped; but we respond to it. It is a miniature example of the rift between our response and the Right that Milton opens in area after area of his poem.

A rather different rift, in the presentation of Hell, has been described by Professor Waldock. In spite of the assurances that it is a place of perpetual punishment, what we are chiefly struck by is 'the atmosphere of busy planning, of life nearly as lively as ever, of energies unquenched'. It is possible to reply that though the devils seem comfortable they are really feeling bad inside (this solution is suggested by 'But the hot Hell that always in him burns' (ix, 467) and similar lines) and that if we hold this in our minds while reading the first two books, the scenes of discussion and amusement will appear as a ghastly pretence. The trouble with this way out is not so much that there are occasional obstacles it will not get us past—if, for instance, 'Suspended Hell' (ii, 554) means what it says, then the torture-without-end account of Hell really must be exaggerated—as that, while we may assume the ghastly pretence, we are not enabled to understand what it feels like. Milton has not made the psychological Hell real. The failure is particularly forced upon us in relation to the feeling of hope. 'Hope never comes' (i, 66) can be believed only if it means hope of some specially authentic kind, different from the 'fallacious' or 'false pretentious' hope of the devils (ii, 521-2, 568). *How* different is left vague. That the hope which never comes should be the kind which 'comes to all' (i, 67) seems to be against making it very special, and certainly 'false' and 'fallacious' cannot mean 'unjustified'—much of what the devils hope for comes about. The difference must be meant to lie in the feeling itself. Conceivably this could be dramatised, but Milton's devils talk as if they feel just ordinary hope, like the rest of us (e.g. ii, 208-25). What we have is an asserted but unexemplified distinction. The same mistiness attaches to Satan's hope. He is said to be 'beyond hope' (ii, 7), and 'farewell Hope' (iv, 107) is put into his mouth. But he tells Gabriel he has hope of finding somewhere to live on earth (iv, 938), tells himself that he hopes to make others miserable (ix, 127, 477), and is so hopeful when he is a snake that his bristles light up (ix, 633-4). Oddly God is the only figure in the poem who cannot hope: his omniscience precludes it.

'Reason', like hope, is a word of unclarified doubleness. Belial's words, we learn, are 'cloth'd in reason's garb' (ii, 226), which implies that they are phoney. But is not 'To suffer, as to do,/Our strength is equal, nor the Law unjust/That so ordains' (ii, 199-201) reasonable by God's standards? Satan claims that 'reason' has made the Son equal to other heavenly creatures, and 'force' has made him supreme (i, 248). We are plainly meant to dismiss the first proposition, but the second is true. God does not trust to reasoning when he elevates the Son (v, 602). It appears that what God calls 'right reason' (vi, 42) is distinguished from wrong reason by its unreasoning obedience to divine ultimatums (about the Son, apples, astronomy, or what not). Right reason has a built-in limit. It is careless of Raphael not to mention this when formulating the poem's official doctrine: 'what obeys/Reason is free, and Reason he made right' (ix, 351-2). 'Right, up to a point' would be safer. The orthodox may reply: 'It is always unreasonable to disobey God'. If 'unreasonable' means 'inadvisable', the poem bears this out, but if God is acknowledged to be above (i.e. different from) reason, then disobeying him and being unreasonable cannot be the same. Adam's reason could not have told him not to eat from one particular tree. God contradicted what reason would have recommended. Milton's rational distrust of mystery is clear on every page of *Christian Doctrine*, and there is a distinct impulse in *Paradise Lost* to make reason and God identical. So the fall, which was disobedience to God, is also presented as disobedience to reason, and this prime irrationality of Adam's is even supposed to have a magical effect, like the opening of Pandora's box, because (here Milton is following St. Augustine) the passions, once let out, can never be properly controlled again (xii, 86–90). But reason and the Hebrew God cannot be equated. The attempt to superimpose them produces a God who reasons but will not be reasoned with and a devil who (with Eve) reasons more brilliantly than God. The introduction of the term '*right* reason' shows Milton squashing the difficulty by mere assertion. But God's resort to force leaves him open to Satan's 'who overcomes/By force, hath overcome but half his foe' (i, 648–9), and this has behind it a truth which would be on the side of any reasonable God. Neither Father nor Son, as Milton presents them, qualifies for Adam's excited praise of a God who overcomes strength with weakness (xii, 565–9).

That Milton's temperament and political beliefs would, if the characters involved had not been God and Satan, have landed him on Satan's side, there is probably no point in denying. But the hugeness of that 'if' left him free to throw all his energies into the depiction of the devils, with no fear of being misunderstood, which is why Mammon sounds like Samson, in preferring 'Hard liberty before the easy yoke/Of servile Pomp' (ii, 256–7), and why Satan, during the temptation (ix, 697–9) seems to be quoting *Areopagitica*. Blake thought Milton was of the devil's party 'without knowing it', but there seems no reason to suppose that the man who created Satan did not realise what a great dramatist his temperament was allowing him to be.

### THE UNIVERSE

In the Middle Ages men imagined the universe as the 2nd-century Alexandrian astronomer Ptolemy had. At its centre was the earth, surrounded by concentric spheres, each of which carried round, as it revolved, a planet (reading outwards from the earth: the moon, Mercury, Venus, the Sun, Mars, Jupiter and Saturn). Beyond Saturn was the sphere in which the fixed stars were stuck. Beyond this was an outer crust (*primum mobile*) which moved the other spheres as it turned round. In the 10th century astronomers introduced another ('Crystalline') sphere, just inside the crust, which wobbled and so explained why their sums came wrong.

It had occurred to ancient thinkers that the earth went round the sun, but the notion was revived, after two thousand years, by the Pole, Copernicus, who published his *Revolutions of the Heavenly Bodies* in 1543. He argues that the sun, the 'spirit, ruler, and visible god of the universe', must lie at its centre, but still believes that the planets (Mercury, Venus, the earth, Mars, Jupiter and Saturn) are fixed to solid revolving spheres. The irregular planetary movements which had worried Ptolemaic astronomers could now be put down to the changing perspective of the earthly observer. The Ptolemaic universe had measured about 20,000 terrestrial radii across. If it were that small, and the earth really did move in an orbit, it was hard to explain why the 'fixed stars' did not appear to move. So Copernicus increased the size of the universe by about 2,000 times, to make the earth's orbit (not just the earth) a mere point compared with the sphere of the fixed stars.

Among English Copernicans, Thomas Digges, whose *Description of the Celestial Orbs* came out in 1576, went even further by denying the existence of the sphere of the fixed stars and arguing that space containing stars extends infinitely upwards. Digges anticipated Giordano Bruno, who developed the theory of an infinite universe containing an infinity of solar systems, and disseminated it throughout Europe. His *Infinite Universe* appeared in 1584. 'Up' and 'down' now became relative terms, and the 'centre' of the universe no longer had any meaning. The Catholic Church scented the threat to its doctrines, and Bruno was burned at the stake in 1600.

There were scientists who dragged their feet as well. The Dane,

Tycho Brahe (1546–1601), invented a compromise universe with the sun and moon going round the earth but everything else going round the sun. But he finally disposed of the planetary 'spheres' by observing that the paths of comets cut through them.

With the coming of the 17th century Copernicus was completely vindicated by the researches of Kepler and Galileo. Kepler (1571–1630) formulated the three laws of planetary motion which served as a basis for Newton's work. Galileo (1564–1642) first peered through his refracting telescope in 1609, and published the astonishing results next year in his *Starry Messenger*, describing the landscape of the moon, mapping all the new stars he had discovered, and announcing that Jupiter had four moons (an upsetting discovery, since it seemed to mean that Jupiter was four times as good as the earth). A more advanced telescope constructed by Huygens in 1655 enabled him to distinguish the ring around Saturn. Technology was now leaping forward to supplement theory, and great observatories began to be built. Louis XIV founded the Royal Observatory of Paris in 1667, and Charles II built Greenwich Observatory, appointing the first Astronomer Royal in 1675.

Into this atmosphere Milton launched a poem which informs astronomers that they are wasting their time and adopts a plan of the universe which had been discarded by serious thinkers for a hundred years: the earth, surrounded by seven planetary spheres, a wobbly crystalline sphere, and a *primum mobile* firm enough for Satan to walk on (iii, 481–3, 418). Satan, who can observe the whole system from above, sees clearly that the earth is its centre (ix, 109), which shows that Raphael is, in the poem's terms, misleading Adam when he mentions the Copernican theory (viii, 121–40). But this, plus other doubts about an earth-circling sun which Milton hints (iii, 574–5; iv, 592–5; x, 668–78), has the effect of making the poem's cosmos seem not just defunct but make-believe. Its *primum mobile* has a hole in the top, for getting in and out, and hangs on a golden chain (ii, 1051) let down from Heaven. Besides the chain, there is a retractable staircase (iii, 523) and (later) a causeway for taking people down to Hell (ii, 1026–7). Above lies Heaven, with its day-and-night machine and its buildings of solid jewellery. Dr. Jackson Cope has argued bravely that it must be spaceless and mysterious because Milton says it is 'undetermined square or round' (ii, 1048). But this means only that Satan cannot make out its shape from where he is. Sin and *The Book of Revelation* know that it is square (x, 381). It is a jumble of Bible scraps and Olympianism ('rubied Nectar flows' (v, 633) when God gives a banquet)— quite lacking Hell's intensity. All around is chaos, which is said to be 'boundless' but seems parochial with its querulous ruler sitting in a tent. Chaos is made of the same stuff as God but is a part of himself from which he has withdrawn his 'goodness', leaving it as the raw material for anything (Hell, Earth) he should wish to make (vii, 166–71).

Professor Lewis explains that when Chaos talks to Satan of 'that side Heav'n from whence your Legions fell' (ii, 1006) it is 'not a mere "poetical periphrasis" for "lower side" or "bottom". These expressions are avoided because there is no up or down in chaos'. He refers us to ii, 893–4 where, sure enough, we are told that chaos is 'Without dimension, where length, breadth, and highth,/And time and place are lost'. But Milton soon talks cheerfully of 'moments' in this timeless non-place (907), and when Satan hits an air-pocket 'down he drops/Ten thousand fadom' (933–4). The kind of chaos Professor Lewis wants is not there. Despite the preliminary brow-knotting, Milton makes his chaos nothing much worse than bad weather. It is the same with Death, who starts out mistily—'That other shape,/If shape it might be call'd that shape had none/Distinguishable' (ii, 666–8)— but within four lines is wearing a crown, and soon has head and hands like anyone else (711–12). This contrast (it happens again with Hell and with God) between mind-boggling attributes and an entity which, when wheeled into the narrative, is quite commonplace, is related, of course, to that rift between what the poem says it is going to be about and the meanings it is able to enforce which, when it involves moral issues, raises our hackles.

Professor Nicolson has called *Paradise Lost* a modern cosmic poem, 'played against a background of interstellar space'. Enthusiasm for this aspect of it is apt to appear self-induced. We know that the light from even the nearest stars takes years to reach the earth, whereas you can drop from top to bottom of Milton's universe in six days (nine for the trip from Heaven to Hell, which is one and a half times the radius of the created universe, i, 73-4; vii, 871). True, when Satan sees the universe as 'a Star/Of smallest Magnitude close by the moon' (ii, 1052-3), it means that either he has been swept badly off-course in chaos, or Milton is tacitly stretching the gap between Heaven and Hell. But as a cosmic poem *Paradise Lost* was obsolete before it was written. Pascal's 'The eternal silence of those infinite spaces fills me with terror' chills more than Milton's whole universe.

## ADAM AND EVE

The poem's official view, that Adam is Eve's superior, is not one which seems likely to a modern reader, or, one suspects, would have convinced a Restoration audience.

The faintly alien impression Adam makes is the result of a collection of circumstances. When he reproaches Eve for running away from him—'Whom fli'st thou? . . . to give thee being I lent/Out of my side to thee, nearest my heart/Substantial life' (iv, 482-5)—the emphasis sounds unfair. 'I lent' makes it seem he volunteered to lose a rib, which is not what he told Raphael, and the anguished overtones of 'nearest my heart' belie the perfectly painless operation he actually underwent (viii, 452-68). There are other irksome moments. One does not expect a 17th-century husband to help with the housekeeping, but Milton gently reveals that Adam has not bothered to find out whether Eve has to store food or can serve it fresh, which besides suggesting incuriosity, puts him at a disadvantage when he starts fixing the menu (v, 314-30). It does not help for Eve to assure Adam that she is lucky to have him: 'I . . . enjoy/So far the happier Lot, enjoying thee/Preeminent by so much odds, while thou/Like consort to thyself canst nowhere find' (iv, 456-8). Masculine complacency pokes out too obviously under the sheep's clothing, and we feel it unfair that Eve should be made to broadcast such theories. Besides, any real husband would be suspicious at once. Eve slips off to look at the garden when she sees from Adam's face that he is 'Ent'ring on studious thoughts abstruse' (viii, 40), and she has our sympathy. Milton is a little too quick in assuring us that she was not bored. His prediction of how Adam would brighten up the lecture on astronomy, 'hee, she knew, would intermix/Grateful digressions, and solve high dispute/With conjugal Caresses' (viii, 54–6), is unenchanting. It is awkward to imagine Adam pulling himself together after each interlude.

St. Augustine thought Adam's mental powers 'surpassed those of the most brilliant philosopher as much as the speed of a bird surpasses that of a tortoise', and C. S. Lewis tells us that we 'must assume' such a being 'before we can read the poem'. But plain sense will tell us that Milton's Adam is not unusually quick-witted. His deductions are unreliable: 'needs must the Power/That made us, and for us this ample World/Be infinitely good' (iv, 412–14)—so might one battery-hen reason with another. When he argues with Eve she soon has him in a tangle. Trying to stop her from risking temptation he puts over the debatable idea that even to withstand temptation is disgraceful: 'hee who tempts, though in vain, at least asperses/The tempted with dishonour foul, suppos'd/Not incorruptible of Faith' (ix, 296–8). He is trying to cover up his real reason for wanting her to avoid temptation, which is that he thinks she might fall (he has misgivings when she has gone). But the tactic he chooses is a poor one, not only because it leaves itself open to Eve's straight rejoinder—'his foul esteem/Sticks no dishonour on our Front, but turns/Foul on himself' (ix, 329–31), but also because it makes his own distrust of her integrity a 'dishonour foul' as well. With his final argument, that Eve should stay with him because there would be no witness to her constancy otherwise (ix, 368–9), he becomes more thoughtless than Eve after the fall, who at least remembers God might have seen (xi, 811–15).

Adam is said to be 'form'd' for 'valour', but he could have had few opportunities for showing it in a world full of tame animals. Eating fruit and pruning were to be the sum of his occupations, neither of them particularly mettlesome. His frightened lie when the Son comes to judge him in the garden—'from her hand I could suspect no ill' (x, 140)—attempts to shift all the punishment on to Eve. It detracts from the favourable impression made by his self-sacrifice at the fall. We see that, when the test comes, 'How can I live without thee' drains away in trembling self-preservation. Watching Adam unmanned in front of his wife is repellent. His earlier confidence that he would be braver when she was looking on (ix, 310–11) now seems pathetic. Some of our disgust rubs off on to the smooth, unnecessary questions with which the Son breaks his culprit down (x, 103–8; 119–23). Eve, on the other hand, conceals from the interrogator her husband's responsibility, as she sees it, for her crime (x, 160–3, compare ix, 1155–7). After Adam's poor showing here we are hardly surprised to find him trying to wheedle some masculine sympathy out of an archangel, and are glad he is snubbed (xi, 632–4).

The speech in which Eve begs Adam's forgiveness—'Forsake me not thus, Adam' (x, 914–36)—is one of the most resplendent human occasions the poem has to show. Suffering, which affects Adam's temper, ennobles her. She offers herself: 'that all/The sentence from thy head remov'd may light/On me, sole cause to thee of all this woe'. Apart from Eve only Christ makes a gesture so total—indeed her words pick up his: compare x, 934–6 with iii, 236–8. Christ, of course, knows that his offer will be accepted. Still, the situation has a compensatory terror for Eve because she has no assurance, as Christ has, that her sacrifice will not be permanent (iii, 242–3). The way Adam receives her speech is not only ungenerous but dishonest. He brushes aside her selflessness with a disparaging counter-claim: 'If Prayers/Could alter high Decrees, I to that place/Would speed before thee, and be louder heard,/That on my head all might be visited' (x, 952–5). The boast exactly contradicts his quivering explanation to the Son as to why he is going to betray his wife: 'Lest on my head both sin and punishment,/However insupportable, be all/Devolv'd' (x, 133–5).

Milton has not been able to make life in Paradise seem happy or beautiful. It has formality without grace. 'Our Grand Parents' deport themselves gravely among its bric-à-brac—'enamell'd colours', 'Sapphire Fount', 'crystal mirror'. The cash-values which dictate the gold ornamentation of Heaven denaturalise

Eden, too, where flowers harden to a 'rich inlay . . . more colour'd than with stone/Of costliest Emblem' (iv, 701–2). Even the apple-peel is gold. There is not a real tree or flower in the place. The grandiose battlements (iv, 543–50) draw attention to the cramped life within, and, like the garden, are sham: the only enemy they have to exclude can jump over the wall at the back (iv, 181). The stately titles Adam and Eve pass back and forth—'My Author and Disposer', 'Daughter of God and Man, accomplisht Eve'—prohibit conversational interplay. The staidness of Milton's Eden shows up bleakly when we put it against a more modern one—Hans Castorp's vision in Thomas Mann's *Magic Mountain*:

> The bright, rainy veil fell away; behind it stretched the sea, a southern sea of deep, deepest blue shot with silver lights, and a beautiful bay, on one side mistily open, on the other enclosed by mountains . . . Youths were at work with horses, running hand on halter alongside their whinnying, head-tossing charges; pulling the refractory ones on a long rein, or else, seated bareback, striking the flanks of their mounts with naked heels, to drive them into the sea. The muscles of the riders' backs played beneath the sun-bronzed skin, and their voices were enchanting beyond words as they shouted to each other or to their steeds. A little bay ran deep into the coast line, mirroring the shore as does a mountain lake; about it girls were dancing. One of them sat with her back toward him, so that her neck, and the hair drawn to a knot above it smote him with loveliness. She sat with her feet in a depression of the rock and played on a shepherd's pipe, her eyes roving above the stops to her companions. . . . Children played and exulted among the breaking waves. A young female, lying outstretched, drawing with one hand her flowered robe high between her breasts, reached with the other in the air after a twig bearing fruit and leaves, which a second, a slender-hipped creature, erect at her head, was playfully withholding . . . A dignity, even a gravity, was held, as it were, in solution in their lightest mood, perceptible only as an ineffable spiritual influence, a high seriousness without austerity, a reasoned goodness conditioning every act. All this, indeed, was not without its ceremonial side. A young mother, in a brown robe loose at the shoulder, sat on a rounded mossy stone and suckled her child, saluted by all who passed with a characteristic gesture which seemed

to comprehend all that lay implicit in their general bearing. . . .
This mixture of formal homage with lively friendliness, and the
slow, mild mien of the mother as well, where she sat pressing her
breast with her forefinger to ease the flow of milk to her baby,
glancing up from it to acknowledge with a smile the reverence paid
her—this sight thrilled Hans Castorp's heart with something very
close akin to ecstasy.

There is a lot here, of course, that Milton could not have used.
But the reconciliation of ceremony with liveliness, the sense we
are given of a purer and freer, yet recognisably human life, the
frank observation of the bared breast—these are aspects that seem
close to his purposes in *Paradise Lost*. Perhaps he could not make
Adam ride a horse, but he does not even run or jump or climb a
tree. He has no muscles (the Michelangelo comparisons sometimes drawn could not be more loose). Though supposedly
young enough to start a family, he and Eve are crushingly
unvivacious. They laugh only once—at an elephant's trunk
(iv, 345–7). According to St. Augustine they could feel no per-
turbation before the fall. Eve's blush (viii, 511) suggests that
Milton is not following this theory, but playfulness is firmly
reserved for sex after the fall (ix, 1027, 1045). Their pre-fall
ignorance of death, which might have made them seem strange
and innocent, is mishandled. 'Whate'er Death is,/Some dreadful
thing no doubt' (iv, 426), says Adam lightheartedly. But it
emerges that he had a shrewd idea all along (x, 809–10), and Eve
can tell a live snake from a dead one without any assistance
(ix, 764).

Though the poem is about the first marriage, the uneasiness
Milton feels on the subject of fecundity is revealed by his making
the vegetation of Eden threateningly exuberant, and giving
Adam and Eve a repressive job —'to lop thir wanton growth', as
Adam puts it (iv, 629)—the sexual 'wanton' combining castrat-
ingly with 'lop' (used elsewhere for the amputation of Dagon's
head and hands, i, 459). It is an informative moment when we
hear Adam approving of nature because she is 'frugal' (viii, 26),
an idea he could not possibly have picked up from his environ-
ment. It is not only reproduction but organic life itself that the

poem shies away from. Its organic images repeatedly register loathing—the masculine volcano (similar in looks to God, see vi, 57–9) with its sulphurous 'womb' (i, 670–4), the 'entrails', 'singed bottom' and 'stench' (i, 234–7), the first miners rifling 'the bowels of thir mother Earth' (i, 687), the phallic cannon embowelling the air and tearing 'all her entrails' (vi, 587–9). Sin is the most violent of the poem's sex-horrors, raped by one son, and chewed internally by the rest (ii, 790–802).

The sexual union the poem feels happiest with is the fleshless one between sun and earth (see, for example, iii, 585, where 'gentle penetration', and v, 300, where the 'mounted' sun bring copulation as near to recognition as it ever gets). Milton did not feel able to describe Adam and Eve's union in these terms. Instead he ushers them out of sight behind a flowery fence (iv, 695–700) and still thinks of Eve as 'virgin' afterwards (ix, 270). Human flesh, although new-created and unfallen, is objectionable enough for Raphael to hold out hopes of Adam and Eve's getting rid of it and achieving gaseous perfection (v, 497)—a suggestion which casts doubt on God's claim that he made them 'just and right' in the first place. Predictably Raphael's low opinion of flesh, but admiration for God, who made it, ends with him tripping himself up. He admits that mankind has to be propagated by 'the sense of touch' (viii 579), and insists that man was created pure (623), yet he obviously considers the sense of touch impure because he says that the angels, though they love without it, still enjoy 'Whatever pure thou in the body enjoy'st' (viii, 622). Adam tells Raphael he felt 'passion' when he went to bed with Eve (viii, 530), and Raphael says that passion is wrong (viii, 588), which leaves Milton in the apparently unique position of maintaining that sex was sinful even before the fall. The wisdom of creating woman at all is obliquely questioned when, near the beginning, the devils dig out 'ribs' which, Milton says, it would have been better to leave where they were (i, 688–90). Angels, it turns out, can assume not only 'either sex' but 'both' (i, 424), with the implication that their gaseous sex-act, expounded by Raphael, can be solitary.

Accordingly when Milton begins to wag his finger over

the nudes: 'Nor those mysterious parts were then conceal'd,/ Then was not guilty shame: dishonest shame/Of Nature's works' (iv, 312–14), we do not believe him sincere for a moment ('mysterious' betrays his embarrassment for a start), and we feel justified in our scepticism when, a little later on, he denounces mixed dancing (iv, 768). His dramatic instinct is surer when he leaves it to Adam to defend human sexuality. It is one of the few times in the poem that we want to applaud. Raphael has been carrying on about how men and women are really just like animals, and Adam, as if in passing, reproves the angel's coarseness—'Though higher of the genial Bed by far,/And with mysterious reverence I deem' (viii, 598–9). Well may Raphael blush.

Adam and Eve, though their nakedness is advertised and preached over, are never looked at steadily. The recurrent references to their hands seem intent on averting our eyes from other areas, and metaphorical drapes are supplied: the bodies are 'clad' in 'naked Majesty' (iv, 289–90) or the 'Robe' of shame (ix, 1058–9). It is not as if physical attraction were supposed to be unimportant to them. They enthuse about each other's charms. But this is simply a part of their experience which Milton is disinclined to block in. The result is that a poem with two naked lovers walking about in it is completely unprovocative. It might be argued that this is a triumph of Milton's art, or at least that he has capitalised on his limitations, and conveyed the purity of pre-fall sex. But the defence will not really work. Milton has not put over the ordinarily provocative details in some new way, so that we see their wholesomeness (as Mann has when he shows the young mother's breast), he has simply refrained from talking about them. We glimpse only one half of one of Eve's breasts, and that is primly screened by her long hair (iv, 495–6). Milton has, though, brilliantly suggested how Eve would look to *l'homme moyen sensuel* by letting Satan's mind wander as he talks to her about the fruit:

> Grateful to appetite, more pleas'd my sense
> Than smell of sweetest Fennel, or the Teats

Of Ewe or Goat dropping with milk at Ev'n,
Unsuckt of Lamb or Kid, that tend thir play.
To satisfy the sharp desire I had
Of tasting those fair Apples. . . .

ix, 580–5

So his eye travels over the naked woman. The theory that Satan cannot feel pleasure (ix, 114–15) wears thin when we watch him in the poem. He is its most sensuously-alive character (God and the angels, like Adam and Eve before the fall (ix, 283), are crippled sensewise because they cannot experience pain). Contrast Satan with the utterly unsusceptible Raphael. When he walks up to the naked woman his eye goes straight to the point: 'Hail Mother of Mankind, whose fruitful Womb/Shall fill the World' (v, 388–9). Eve stands there, lets him look, and does not so much as colour (384–5). This is innocence: frank, functional. It is a limpid moment (and would be finer still if one did not suspect a cruel pun on 'fruitful'). Eve is, admittedly, not without a sugar-coating ('coy' (iv, 310) hardly sounds bravely innocent), but we should beware of thickening this unwarrantably. Professor Peter is disarmed by the modesty which moves Eve 'to postpone for a little their nuptial rites by drawing out the "gentle purpose" of their conversation (iv, 641–58)'. But his pleasure is extra-textual. The stage-direction 'Thus talking hand in hand alone they pass'd/On to their blissful Bower' (iv, 689–90) suggests that Eve is not trying to hold up the proceedings, but just filling in time until they can be out of sight of the animals. When Milton arrives at the consummation, his touch fails. The lovers:

Straight side by side were laid, nor turn'd I ween
Adam from his fair Spouse, nor Eve the Rites
Mysterious of connubial Love refus'd.

iv, 741–3

'I ween' sounds disastrously as if it comes with a dig in the ribs from one of the more knowing wedding guests, and when Milton passes straight on to an explanation of how perfectly correct it is to satisfy one's bodily desires in this way, the bower is replaced by a lecture-room. It is evident that he has no inkling how to communicate what Adam and Eve are undergoing with any degree of sensuous potency. Calling marriage a 'Perpetual Fountain of Domestic sweets' (760) does not raise it above confectionery. The failure is an outcome of Milton's temperament, not his theories. There is nothing wrong with sensuousness in theory: even God likes music (v, 626–7) and (as in the Bible) has to have prayers mixed with incense before he is prepared to snuff them up (xi, 24–38). But richly sensuous bits tend to be linked with evil, as when God becomes strident about the hellhounds and their 'suckt and glutted offal' (x, 630–3), or the devils chew 'bitter Ashes, which th'offended taste/With spattering noise rejected' (x, 566–7).

## THE FALL

Some critics aver that Adam and Eve must have been sinful before they ate the apple, otherwise Eve would not have admired her own reflection (iv, 461–6) and Adam would not have let her go gardening by herself. Milton forestalls these objections by telling his readers plainly that Eve is 'yet sinless' when she arrives at the tree with the snake (ix, 659), and by making Adam's behaviour distinctly parallel God's. Though Eve is his inferior, Adam leaves her free, as God left him; 'beyond this', as Adam explains, 'had been force,/And force upon free Will hath here no place' (ix, 1173–4). That is how God argued. What is more, God gives Adam to understand, just before he creates Eve, that she is going to be a suitable companion for him only because, unlike the animals, she has a free spirit (viii, 440–3). If, after that, Adam had forcibly detained her, we should have grounds for thinking him already fallen.

Satan's masterstroke in the temptation of Eve is telling her that he has eaten from the tree himself, and found himself able to speak (ix, 599–600). Milton's Eve is astounded to hear a snake talk (ix, 553–4), as the commentators on *Genesis*, including Calvin, had said she must have been. She has no reason to be afraid of snakes: on the contrary, Raphael was perversely careful to inform her husband that they were 'not noxious', even if they looked it (vii, 498). Eve's fall, it might seem then, was perfectly rational. She was deprived of a crucial bit of evidence—the harmfulness of snakes, resulting from their aptness as devilish overcoats—but with the facts at her disposal, her intellect could not but have found 'Reason' and 'Truth' in Satan's words (ix, 737). This view would make her sin a failure not of intellect but of faith: she allowed herself, faithful to her reason, to distrust God. It was the standard Protestant theory, championed by Luther and Calvin, that Eve's first sin was unbelief. When, though, one reads the hundred and thirty lines on which the whole fate of mankind turns—from the moment Eve is said to be 'yet sinless' to the moment she puts out her hand for the apple (ix, 658–780)—one sees that Eve, in the last resort, is not obeying her intellect but trying to suppress it: rationalising, not reasoning: 'What fear I then, rather what know to fear/Under this ignorance of Good and Evil,/Of God or Death, of Law or Penalty?' (ix, 773–5). It is patent self-deception—and it had to be, because Milton, having decided to enthrone reason beside the Hebrew God, could not make Eve's fall really reasonable. We are shown an Eve undermined by flattery and impelled by ambition, curiosity and hunger (ix, 732–4, 740, 743, 790). She is not the Eve of the Protestant theologians but a medieval figure, committing gluttony, avarice and vainglory, the three sins traditionally squeezed out of *Genesis* iii, 6 ('the woman saw that the tree was good for food, and that it was pleasant to the eyes, and a tree to be desired to make one wise'). Mr. Burden maintains that the fatal tree attracts Eve's senses 'only after it has been desired'—vainglory precedes gluttony, and this would make her a bit more of a Renaissance Eve. But Milton's words, 'Fixt on the Fruit she gaz'd, which to behold/Might tempt alone' (ix, 735–6), where 'alone' must mean 'even without Satan tempting at all', put the sensuous content of the temptation very high. Besides, Mr. Burden has left out of account Eve's dream, in which the tree's 'pleasant savoury smell' had 'So quick'n'd appetite, that I, methought,/Could not but taste' (v, 84–6). The provocative qualities of the tree had been rankling in Eve's consciousness before she met the snake at all.

After her fall, Eve decides to share the apple, in case it should turn out to be poisonous (ix, 826–31). Later she assures Adam that she would not let him touch it if she had any doubts (ix, 977–80). The two passages are often indignantly held up as evidence of her bad faith, and at this juncture C. S. Lewis cries murder. But Milton's dramatic handling is delicate enough to outwit violent reactions. Between Eve's two speeches Adam has revealed his intention of dying with her. There is nothing to stop us reading her reply as a corresponding generosity, prompted by his. If anything, that is the conclusion the text favours: 'she embrac'd him, and for joy/Tenderly wept, much won that he his Love/Had so ennobl'd' (ix, 990–2).

Adam falls for love: that had been a commonplace since the middle ages. 'If the reader', says Professor Lewis, 'finds it hard to look upon Adam's action as a sin at all, that is because he is not really granting Milton's premises.' But if he does not find it hard to look upon it as a sin, he is not reading Milton's poem. It was one of Milton's premises that it was 'hard' to be a Christian. In that he was not unusual. Bunyan's Christian has to stuff his fingers in his ears to keep out the screams of his wife and children as he scampers off to save his soul. That is what Adam 'ought' to have done, but in coming to this conclusion we have one bleak monosyllable 'bad' alone on our side (ix, 994), and Adam's reasons against us:

> with thee
> Certain my resolution is to Die;
> How can I live without thee, how forgo
> Thy sweet Converse and Love so dearly join'd,
> To live again in these wild Woods forlorn?
> Should God create another Eve, and I
> Another Rib afford, yet loss of thee
> Would never from my heart; no no, I feel
> The Link of Nature draw me: Flesh of Flesh,
> Bone of my Bone thou art, and from thy State
> Mine never shall be parted, bliss or woe.
>
> ix, 906–16

Mr. Burden thinks that Adam does not value the 'solace and mutual comfort' he enjoys with Eve as much as her body, and so would be Miltonically right to divorce her (supposing he wanted to). Adam's flesh-and-bone emphasis, though, which presumably upsets Mr. Burden, seems rather an allusion to the fact that Eve was made out of him than to the fun they have in bed. After all Adam has just been calling the qualities which the intellect perceives in Eve 'Holy' and 'divine' (898–9), and though the poem's theory is against him here, as when he calls her 'last and best/Of all God's works' (896–7), the idea sounds respectably unphysical. If Mr. Burden wanted to press his point he would have to argue that 'converse' could mean 'sexual intercourse' as well as 'conversation' in the 17th century (it could, in fact), and that this, with the suspiciously copulative force of 'join'd' (which Bentley, Milton's 18th-century editor, felt awkward enough about to change to 'joy'd' (i.e. enjoyed)), just shows what a one-track mind Adam had. When we try to give the words these values, though, we are conscious that we are contaminating the soliloquy. Had Milton shown us a God we could feel it worth sacrificing Eve for, of course, he would have left us a way out, but he has firmly refused to, and we find that we are all Adams as a result.

Christian critics argue that even if Adam's sacrifice seems noble it was certainly futile—he can do no good to Eve, and in fact does none, by becoming her accomplice. But is this true? Had she alone eaten, God was pledged to kill her, and at once (vii, 544). Adam, by saving her from separate punishment, may have saved her life. It is more of a question whether he did any harm by becoming her accomplice. Nature had already given 'signs of woe/That all was lost' (ix, 783–4).

The results of the fall, in *Paradise Lost*, do not accord with Milton's beliefs outlined in *Christian Doctrine*. Milton believed, with St. Augustine, that the tree was harmless. Had it not been forbidden, Adam and Eve could have eaten without risk, and their reason would not have warned them against it. Had the forbidden act been unreasonable, abstention would have proved only reason, not obedience. God's prohibition, says Milton, was based on 'what is called positive right, whereby God, or anyone invested with lawful power, commands or forbids what is in itself neither good nor bad'. But the *Paradise Lost* tree is not harmless. It makes you feel drunk, lecherous, and low the next morning (ix, 793, 1008, 1013, 1046–54). Even had God picked another tree for his obedience-test it would have been unkind of him not to warn them off this one. The consequent dramatic impact is immense. We can never think of the two lovers in the same way again when we have seen them leering tipsily at each other (ix, 1013–15). But it is Milton who has, so to speak, been tampering with their drinks, and in a way which, he knows, contradicts his beliefs (what he seems to be remembering is the rabbinic notion that the tree of knowledge was the vine). The theory to which the poem actually subscribes is not that the apple is alcoholic but that by one act of disobedience man unaccountably turns on a psychological stopcock in himself which he is never able to turn off again, so ever afterwards his reason is at the mercy of his passions (ix, 1122–31; xii, 83–90). In *Christian Doctrine* Milton makes this sorcerer's-apprentice psychology sound likely by explaining that it is natural for one sin to lead to 'gross and habitual sin'. But dramatising the sudden change would be a much more difficult matter, and Milton has shirked it. He unwarrantably drugs his apple in order to degrade his characters from outside, instead of showing them spoiled internally.

*[handwritten margin note: reason now at mercy of Adam's (man's) passions.]*

*[handwritten margin note: yet does suggest that internal degradation in one's vanity from the start.]*

## STYLE

As sage, though not as hero, Milton was above the epic. His Stoicism required an audience 'fit' but 'few' (vii, 31), and those few, as he stipulated in the preface to his anti-Royalist tract *Eikonoklastes*, of 'such value and substantial worth, as truth and wisdom, not respecting numbers and bigg names, have bin ever wont in all ages to be contented with'. This speaker could have little in common with his narrator, Raphael, whose respect for numbers and big names is patent ('Attended with ten thousand thousand saints . . . And twenty thousand (I thir number heard)/ Chariots' (vi, 767–80), is Raphael's level). It is particularly in Raphael's account of the war that we sense the inflation that has attracted so much criticism to Milton's style in our century.

Later, correcting Adam's simple notions about the universe, Raphael momentarily takes a higher tone—'Consider first, that Great/Or Bright infers not Excellence' (viii, 90–1). But if so, it is indeed a question why the poem makes so much of angels being bigger than men, or of God and his Son looking so bright, as if they were superior types of electric bulb.

Since there is this divided attitude in Milton himself, it is not surprising that the style is in places hollow. The writing is weakest when he tries to scrape elevation out of an extinct tradition like allegory, as in the list of Chaos's courtiers:

> Orcus and Ades, and the dreaded name
> Of Demogorgon; Rumour next and Chance,
> And Tumult and Confusion all imbroil'd,
> And Discord with a thousand various mouths.
>
> ii, 964–7

The lame 'all imbroil'd' sounds as if Milton is tired of it himself. At the other extreme of intensity one could take the geographical passages—the Chinese wind-waggons (iii, 438–9), for example, or the Arabian spice-routes (iv, 159–65)—which transfuse Milton's excitement about travel-books into his poem, or the descriptions of blindness—the crushing softness of the verb in 'So thick a drop serene hath quencht thir Orbs' (iii, 25).

It has been argued that wallowing in the Miltonic sound stops one noticing what the words mean; but equally the splendour of the noise has often a serious point to make. Take, for instance: 'or aggravate/His sad exclusion from the doors of Bliss' (iii, 524–5). This, we suspect, even as we roll it over our tongues, pitches one of the poem's meanest acts too sonorously high. But consider it from Satan's angle, and the incongruity disappears. For him God's little trick is truly terrible. In the creation-account, especially, the sound can be strictly graphic. The little fish which 'Glide under the green Wave' (vii, 401) are nimbler than the big ones 'Wallowing unwieldly, enormous in thir Gait' (vii, 411), because the syllables ripple in one line and lumber in the other.

This last example may make Milton seem too much like Pope.

In reality he represents a final protest against the settling down of poetic style into Augustanism. He claimed divine inspiration, at a time when Hobbes was coolly wondering why a man 'enabled to speak wisely from the principles of nature and his own meditation' should wish 'to be thought to speak by inspiration, like a Bagpipe'. To Dr. Johnson, Milton's diction amounted to a deformity: 'Of him, at last may be said what Jonson says of Spenser, that *he wrote no language*, but has formed what Butler calls a *Babylonish dialect*, in itself harsh and barbarous'. And post-Augustan critics have blamed Milton for not exploiting the thew and sinew of English. But if we compare Nashe's prose, at the end of the 16th century, with Dryden's, or Donne's poetry with Waller's, we shall see that literary English had no thew or sinew left when Milton wrote his epic. What it desperately needed was toughness and intricacy, and these Milton's syntactical and linguistic daring reintroduced.

Coleridge called Milton's word-order and connection of sentences 'exquisitely artificial', and noticed that the positioning, as in Greek and Latin, obeys 'the logic of passion or universal logic' rather than 'the logic of grammar'. Milton makes grammar flexible and disappoints or outgoes our expectations. When Adam says 'both Death and I/Am found Eternal' (x, 815–16), his realisation that death and he now obscenely inhabit the same body is pushed out at the reader by the ungrammatically singular verb. The shout of joy in heaven shows another kind of ungrammar (called *anacoluthon* in rhetorical text-books):

> No sooner had th'Almighty ceas't, but all
> The multitude of Angels with a shout
> Loud as from numbers without number, sweet
> As from blest voices, uttering joy, Heav'n rung
> With Jubilee, and loud Hosannas fill'd
> Th'eternal Regions.
>
> iii, 344–9

R. M. Adams bends the passage to make it grammatical, taking 'multitude' as subject, 'rung' as verb and 'Heav'n' as object. Bentley had a less ugly solution: 'Here's a Sentence without a

Verb', he said, and changed it to 'gave a shout'. But Milton has left the structure open-ended. The shout hangs in the air, re-echoing, passing into clamorous Hosannas. Milton is thinning his grammar like paint, and paints the shout. One's attention is often drawn to niceties of syntax by Bentley's destruction of them. When Satan first sees chaos, for instance: 'Into this wild Abyss the wary fiend/Stood on the brink of Hell and look'd a while' (ii, 917–18). 'Here's an absurd and ridiculous Blunder,' says Bentley, 'Satan "Stood into" the Abyss . . . He did not stand into it, but stood on the firm ground, the Brink of Hell'—accordingly the second line gets altered to 'Look'd from the brink of Hell, and stood a while'. Of course Bentley is right about the grammar: it does mean 'Stood, and looked into', but with his rewriting the vertiginous tilt of 'Stood into', as Satan peers over the edge, never happens.

An absence of metaphor has been alleged in *Paradise Lost*, and interpreted as an effort to restore the innocency of primitive vision, seeing spades as spades. This theory cannot comfortably account for Milton's big similes, or for his oxymorons—'precious bane', 'darkness visible', 'sweet compulsion', 'stupidly good', which reflect the poem's conflict between theory and impact. 'A circling row/Of goodliest Trees loaden with fairest Fruit' (iv, 146–7) exemplifies the metaphor-less mode, but even without metaphor Milton usually avoids this straightforwardness. There is, for instance, nothing metaphoric about 'liquid Lapse of murmuring Streams' (viii, 263): indeed, what rejuvenates the phrase is the literal-instead-of-figurative use of 'lapse' (new in this line, according to the *OED*). This use of a word derived from Latin in its Latin sense has been said to be un-English (and so bad), but Milton does not shut out the pressure of the English sense, and when this, by contrast or any way else, can be absorbed to enrich the whole, he makes the language more resourceful, not less. To take a simple case, when Satan 'on the Coast averse/From entrance or Cherubic Watch' (ix, 67–8) enters Paradise, the Latin, purely prepositional 'averse', meaning roughly 'opposite', easily embraces, too, its English meaning and Satan's hatred of angels. When Sin and Death construct a passage

'Smooth, easy, inoffensive down to Hell' (x, 305), 'inoffensive' is not there so much for what, via Latin, it means ('free of stumbling-blocks') as for the horrible innocence in which its English sense bathes it. Another specimen comes when snake-Satan talks to Eve, 'erect/Amidst his circling Spires, that on the grass/Floated redundant' (ix, 501–3). Here the primary, Latin sense of 'redundant' ('like waves') is practically eclipsed by the English ('superfluous, unnecessary'), since Satan's upspringing energy is so marked round about by words like 'tow'r'd' and 'Crested aloft' (498, 500) and by the simile of hovering fire (633–42), as well as by the 'Spires' which merely float on top of the grass, that it takes little imagination to see that Satan is not sitting back on his coils but almost leaving the ground with excitement. The process can work in reverse: 'rapture', for instance, came into English with a physical sense near to the Latin *rapio* ('snatch, tear'), and it was Milton, in the *Nativity Ode*, who developed the modern meaning ('ecstasy'). So when he writes about the savage crowd that 'tore' Orpheus limb from limb 'in Rhodope, where Woods and Rocks', which he had been able to charm with his music, 'had Ears/To rapture, till the savage clamour drown'd/Both harp and voice' (vii, 34–7), we do not know whether 'To rapture' means 'while they were enraptured by his music' (in which case it would be a look into the past), or 'to the sound of Orpheus being torn (his shrieks, etc.)'. More simply, Milton writes about the 'bought smile' of prostitutes in the fallen world, and their 'Casual fruition' (iv, 765–7), where the Latin meaning of 'Casual' (related to a fall, *casus*) alertly glosses the English, just as the 'fruit' element protrudes from the word 'fruition'.

'Fruit' is one of the recurrent words that thread through the poem gathering significance and casting a calculated light into innocent contexts—'woe', 'hand', 'tree', 'fall' and 'taste' are others. For instance, when we see Adam and Eve in Paradise 'reaping immortal fruits of joy and love' (iii, 67) we have a preliminary shudder, and the 'Mists and Exhalations' which 'Rising or falling still advance his [God's] praise' (v, 191) are, we realise, doing a little mime of the *felix culpa*—the fall which, in God's great plan, turned out for the best and advanced his glory.

There is an admitted shortage of precise visual images, but not of precise sensory images. The popular defence of Milton's 'epic generality'—that it leaves each reader free to do his own imagining—confuses the two. When Milton writes:

> So from the root
> Springs lighter the green stalk, from thence the leaves
> More aery, last the bright consummate flow'r
> Spirits odorous breathes. . . .

v, 479–82

no plant is seen, but its mass is registered as accurately as any picture could record size and shape. What we have is a weight-picture. The bulky 'consummate', balanced on the flower, seems too heavy, but 'Spirits' and 'breathes' keep it fuming into the air, and we recognise that Milton is getting across the contrast between the precarious size of the petals relative to the stalk, and their filmy lightness. The reader is not left to himself at all, though he may seem to be because the constraints are not the accustomed pictorial ones.

Milton is adept at picking on the aspect of a situation that will give it this sensory dimension: the crabs 'in *jointed* Armour' (vii, 409); Satan like a mountain 'Half sunk *with all his pines*' (vi, 189); the fig-tree, 'a Pillar'd shade/High overarch't, *and echoing Walks between*' (ix, 1106–7). The italicised words, in each case, push depth into the image. Bentley altered the lines from the war in heaven, 'They pluckt the seated Hills with all thir load,/ Rocks, Waters, Woods' (vi, 644–5), to read 'Rocks, Quarries, Woods', because he said the waters would drop out of the bottom when the hills were carried. But it is precisely the vista of lakes still there with woods around them that makes the hills more than dummies. Vagueness is itself enlisted to this end. Death's sniff is an example: 'So scented the grim Feature, and upturn'd/ His Nostril wide into the murky Air' (x, 279–80). Has Death, we are left unpleasantly wondering, only *one* nostril (the singular is not used anywhere else in the poem)? Rapid sensory contrasts also set the imagination working: 'fleecy star' (iii, 558), 'feather'd mail' (v, 284), or 'tore the Thracian Bard' (vii, 34), where the abrupt verb thuds so sickeningly into the stately title.

There are some effects which we will search for without success. The style cannot adapt tone of voice to fit dramatic circumstances very closely. Professor Peter complains that Satan's first speech, though it has some grammatical disjunction, does not sound like a creature being burned alive. Immediacy is lost, and this criticism is only rephrased if we say that we should not look for dramatic realism in an epic. Shifts of emphasis repay scrupulous attention for all that. The doubtful weight Milton will rest on words is beautifully felt in the ending: 'They hand in hand with wand'ring steps and slow,/Through Eden took thir solitary way.' 'Why *wand'ring*?' demanded Bentley. 'Very improper: when in the Line before they were *guided by Providence*.' Exactly; and the contradiction lights up for the last time the fatal permissiveness of Providence. 'And why *thir solitary way*? . . . When even their former Walks in Paradise were as solitary?' They weren't, in fact—a new separation has come between man and nature, man and angel—but what Bentley really misses is the joining force of 'solitary'. The two are truly one, now that Adam has sacrificed God for her. And the ambiguity of 'Eden' (sometimes, up to now, the whole district, but sometimes the garden), plus memories of them 'Imparadis'd' in one another's arms, suddenly opens up for us a glad view of them walking on through Paradise, not turned out at all, but leaving the prison-garden and its baleful faces behind. With this, their wandering steps suddenly look like delight, not dejection: they loiter, enthralled. The world is all before them. A more difficult example comes when the good angels begin to surround Satan:

> With ported Spears, as thick as when a field
> Of Ceres ripe for harvest waving bends
> Her bearded Grove of ears, which way the wind
> Sways them; the careful Plowman doubting stands
> Lest on the threshing floor his hopeful sheaves

> Prove chaff. On th'other side Satan alarm'd
> Collecting all his might dilated stood.

iv, 980–6

The ploughman's worry suggests that Gabriel is not sure his angels will come up to scratch; Satan is alarmed because he thinks they will. What dramatises the passage is that the verbs 'waving bends' and 'sways' can be read to justify either reaction. If they add up to 'swing backwards and forwards' ('which way the wind . . . .' meaning 'whichever way the wind happens to . . .'), then the angels are still carrying their spears upright ('ported') and wavering, which is Gabriel's impression. But if there is really a gale in the field of corn strong enough to blow the ears out, which is what the ploughman suspects, then the spears are fiercely levelled; 'waving bends' means 'first waves, then points one way' (this is the moment the spears come down from the port position); 'sways' has its meaning 'weighs down'; and 'which way the wind . . .' is the Latin construction, 'in that one direction in which the wind . . .'. This is how Satan, alarmed, sees it.

The slapstick war in Heaven can be debited to the classical tradition: epics were meant to have battles. There are other places where Milton tries to bring aboard a classical effect for which there is no room. When Satan first flies in Hell, 'incumbent on the dusky Air/That felt unusual weight' (i, 226–7), we can see that Milton is coveting the superb moment in *Aeneid* vi when Aeneas steps into the boat which ferries dead souls over the Styx: 'The seamy craft groaned under the weight, and through its chinks took in a marshy flood' (413–14), but he has no use to put it to. Virgil's contrast between wispy souls and solid hero corresponds to nothing in Milton's situation: Hell's air has not felt any weight at all before. On the other hand, images can be taken out of Virgil and improved. In Virgil's underworld (and Dante's hell) the souls are compared to 'the leaves of the forest that at autumn's first frost dropping fall' (*Aeneid* vi, 309–10). The idea being conveyed is the large number of leaves (and souls). Milton's fallen angels, lying 'Thick as

Autumnal Leaves that strow the Brooks/In Vallombrosa, where th'Etrurian shades/High overarch't imbow'r' (i, 302–4), are in an 'inflamed Sea', and that difference brings suggestively into the comparison the autumnal leaf-colours flickering on the water.

A factor, finally, which activates the whole framework of *Paradise Lost* is argumentative drive. When Milton lectures on angelic digestion, or the good angels spread out to make the gaps in Heaven less noticeable (vii, 162), or the Creator apologises to Adam for the absence of fish at the naming-ceremony, 'since they cannot change/Thir element to draw the thinner Air' (viii, 347–8), we should feel that we are in contact not with isolated gaucheries but with the cogs of a fierce literalism which powers the poem's intransigent God and Satan, and scores its sturdy stylistic triumphs in lines like: 'The savoury pulp they chew, and in the rind/Still as they thirsted scoop the brimming stream' (iv, 335–6). The objection to some modern interpretations of *Paradise Lost* which view it simply (or, to be fairer, complicatedly) as a spatial diagram in which upward movement is 'good' and downward 'bad' is not so much that they will not fit consistently (Dr. Cope, for instance, maintains that spaciousness is evil and circumscription good, when the one character to use the word 'uncircumscribed' (vii, 170) is God, of himself), nor only that by substituting space for morality they simplify the poem's moral questions, as that they ignore the argumentative fibres which fill it with energy.

# 8

## *Paradise Regained*: The Anti-Epic

Milton could never bear to hear *Paradise Lost* preferred to *Paradise Regained*. It is easy to see why. *Paradise Lost* bristles so irresistibly with questions because by its own moral standards it is a failure. It contains nothing to encourage Adam's belief in a God who overcomes 'worldly strong' by 'things deemed weak' (xii, 567–8). Satan, who prefers guile to force, qualifies for this description better than Milton's Zeus-and-Yahweh hybrid. The advertised 'better fortitude/Of Patience' (ix, 31–2) never materialises. Milton thought of *Paradise Regained* as a 'brief epic' (like the *Book of Job*), but it shakes off classical epic values (power, beauty) which *Paradise Lost* was perfectly happy with. It has nothing as adolescent as the war in Heaven. Its anti-hero, it is eager to point out, is a nobody, with lower-class friends (ii, 27, 81). He is so outmatched physically that the devil can pick him up and hurl him through the air, but he wins by nerve and intellect. The dangerous passions of *Paradise Lost*'s God, skulking 'amidst/Thick clouds and dark' (*PL* ii, 264), are shifted to Satan at the outset ('Within thick Clouds and dark tenfold involv'd, i, 41).

The bleak style announces the new temper. Sentences are briefer; lines more frequently monosyllabic; similes scarce (one per book is the usual ration: i, 452; ii, 155–6; iii, 221–2). We are in Reason's stony land: the stylistic oases (the banquet, the panoramas) are Satan's territory. Christ's manner becomes increasingly brusque (see, for instance, iv, 171 and 485–6).

### THE DETECTIVE ELEMENT
It was a popular idea with theologians long before Milton wrote

that Satan's temptations were detective-work. He was out to discover who Christ was. In his opening speech Milton's Satan tells the devils that Christ is the 'Woman's seed' who (according to what God said in *Genesis* iii, 15) is destined to 'bruise' his head. He reminds them that they had their suspicions about this when Christ was born (i, 66). Now that he has heard God's voice from the clouds announcing Christ 'Son of God' (i, 32, 85), he says flatly that the destined bruiser has arrived (i, 64–5). There is no reason why he should be so sure. God did not say that the 'Woman's seed' would be his son. But it is part of Satan's worry that he is cut off from dependable sources of information and has to make do with guesses. His pessimism may be a scheme to make his followers jumpy. We notice that though he talks gloomily to them of his 'fear', it was not fear but envy and rage that he really felt when he heard the baptismal announcement (i, 38). He may put on 'looks aghast and sad' for this speech because if the devils are thoroughly upset first, his victory will seem all the more splendid (compare *PL* ii, 430–41). At the end of his speech he is guardedly optimistic about his chances of winning (i, 104–5), and Milton later tells us that defeat was the last thing he expected (iv, 11). He begins to have doubts only after the first encounter (ii, 147), but even then feels 'anger' and 'disdain' for the mere man who opposes him (i, 466), not fear.

When he first heard about the 'bruise' he was greatly tickled— 'A World who would not purchase with a bruise?' (*PL*, x, 500). Now it seems less funny, but still ambiguous. He tells the devils it means a 'fatal wound', but implies almost in the same breath it may be just a travel-restriction (i, 53, 60–3). Left alone, he suspects, but only suspects, that 'bruise' is a euphemism for the end of his reign on earth, and that Christ is going to administer it (i, 125). After his first brush with Christ he goes back and tells the devils, 'such an Enemy/Is ris'n to invade us, who no less/ Threat'ns than our expulsion down to Hell' (ii, 126–8). Christ has not threatened this. Either Satan is being a wily alarmist again, or is so perplexed that his suspicions thicken uncontrollably. He has no idea, so far as we can tell, that Christ is the person who drove him out of Heaven. 'His first-begot we know, and sore have felt,/When his fierce thunder drove us to the deep;/Who this is we must learn' (i, 89–91), makes a confident distinction (though it might betray a subconscious association). When he tries to oil his way into Christ's confidence—'But thou art plac't above me, thou art Lord' (i, 475)—it cannot occur to him that he is telling the plain truth for once, otherwise it would be impossible to explain his amazement when Christ finally gets the better of him on the pinnacle. As a matter of fact even the good angels do not seem to understand that this human Son of God is the same as the other one. God tells them 'smiling' (presumably because he has something up his sleeve) that this is a 'man' who is 'call'd' the Son of God (i, 129–55), and they must be misled, because they reply that this new Son's virtue is 'untried'—which they could scarcely say about the victor of the war in Heaven (i, 176). Only at the poem's end can we be sure that they have realised what has happened (iv, 596–609).

Christ does not really know who he is himself. He has no recollection of what happened back in Heaven, because he has to patch together bits from the Bible and his mother's reminiscences before it occurs to him that he is the Messiah (i, 229–67). He does not know why he is having to go into the wilderness, but his ignorance does not worry him: 'what concerns my knowledge God reveals' (i, 293). This is sometimes taken to mean, 'God (or my Divine Half) will slip me information supernaturally when I need it'. But if it meant that, it would destroy the parallel between Christ's ordeal and that of Adam and Eve (or Job) which the poem constantly prompts. We must take it that Christ means, 'What I know is presumably all I need to know at present, otherwise God would let me find out more'. It is a confession of faith, not of a supernatural conspiracy. Milton's Christ is emphatically a 'perfect man' (i, 166), just like Adam. He does not reach his conclusions by magic but by using his head and remembering his Bible. If it were otherwise, God would not have produced, as he boasts he is going to, a 'man' able to resist Satan (i, 150–2).

So, whereas Eve failed to be put on her guard by a talking snake, Christ (to take the instance that looks most like magic) pierces a less suspect disguise by spotting inconsistencies in what the 'aged man in Rural weeds' says. Though this old man is himself alone, he expresses amazement at seeing another solitary man, and alleges that no one has ever survived such a situation (i, 321-5). When Christ remains calm, he asserts with suspicious vehemence that it would be a miracle if one were able to find one's way back to civilisation (i, 337), yet he has just been describing how he and the other inhabitants visit nearby towns and villages (i, 331-2). He draws attention to this blunder, which contradicts his pretence that they are miles even from the nearest caravan route (i, 322-3), by hastily correcting himself—'Town or Village nigh (nighest is far)' (i, 332). Having carelessly revealed that he actually 'saw and heard' Christ's baptism (i, 330), he adds, by way of explanation, that news does filter through to the desert-dwellers, and that they pick up a certain amount in the border-settlements (i, 333-4). But if he was an eyewitness, this explanation is beside the point; it sounds like anxiety to cover up an odd coincidence. The old man plainly exaggerates the food-shortage. Why should the locals need to live on 'roots and stubs' when the area supports a varied animal population (i, 310-13, 339)? He is disguised as a shepherd, and the place looks fit for sheep-farming to Christ (ii, 287). The claim that they are 'to thirst inur'd/More than the Camel', besides its inherent unlikeliness, appears unreasonable when the nightly dew is so heavy that one has to shelter from it (i, 305-7, 339-40; iv, 406). Christ has the first-class detective's brain which Satan needs, and by the time the old man has finished three sentences, has worked out that he is an impostor (i, 348), analysed his motive (i, 355), and picked out the likeliest suspect from the police-records (in this case from the *Book of Job*, which he has read so closely that he is able to reconstruct the feelings of the characters concerned; compare i, 410-26 with *Job* i, 6-12). He tests his deductions with a piece of bluff: 'Why dost thou then suggest to me distrust,/ Knowing who I am, as I know who thou art?' (i, 354-5). It works, and Satan comes clean (i, 358-61). 'Knowing who I am' may mean just 'Knowing I am called the Son of God (you heard it announced)'. But more probably Christ has deduced from

Satan's probing tactics that he does *not* know quite who he is dealing with (he does not realise it is someone whose trust in God is incorruptible, for instance). This makes Christ's bluff perfectly innocent: 'You know who I am only as I know who you are (i.e. approximately)'.

The other moments at which Christ proves unexpectedly knowing require nothing more magical on his part than a rapid intelligence and a mastery of Old Testament prophecies, plus a capacity for keeping calm. He is interested, but not alarmed, to discover that something strange is happening to his alimentary system. At his first encounter with Satan he is still supernaturally unhungry: he hungers 'first', Milton says, at ii, 244. (This makes bread-from-stones less of a temptation: Milton clouds the issue by mentioning before the temptation the hunger Christ is going to feel after it, i, 308–9.) But once God lets him feel hunger, Christ observes his own symptoms as clinically as a scientist with a new drug. 'Now I feel I hunger' has the correctly detached tone, and he concludes, after finding no signs of emaciation, that his organism can function without food (ii, 252–7). As a result he is a step ahead of Satan, who still thinks hunger 'life's enemy' a hundred lines later (ii, 373–4).

Christ's reply to the Satanic banquet, 'I can at will, doubt not, as soon as thou,/Command a Table in this Wilderness,/ And call swift flights of Angels ministrant/Array'd in Glory on my cup to attend' (ii, 383–6), has often been taken as a flash of inspiration, but he could quite well have worked it out for himself. As often, he is half-quoting the Old Testament—*Psalm* lxxviii, 19, where the distrustful Jews say, 'Can God furnish a table in the wilderness?' The answer was yes, of course; and if desert-catering was not beyond God, a Miltonic Christ could deduce that it was not beyond him. He had read prophecies of himself like *Isaiah* xl, 3: 'the voice of him that crieth in the wilderness, Prepare ye the way of Jehovah; make straight in the desert a highway for our God' (this is the version of the text Milton quotes in *Christian Doctrine*), and could infer from this, as Milton does, either that he was Jehovah himself (the wrong answer, says Milton), or that Jehovah's power was resident in him if he chose to use it. 'As soon as thou' (ii, 383) is, besides, infuriatingly guarded from Satan's angle. He cannot command flights of angels at all.

In the same way Christ's prophecy of his world-wide kingdom (iv, 146–51), which permits him to claim that everything Satan offers is his own already (iv, 191), is simply a recitation from *Daniel* ii, 31–5 and iv, 10–12. Biblical scholars had always interpreted these visions of Nebuchadnezzar as prophecies of Christ's kingdom. Christ knows, too, from scrutiny of the relevant texts, that his kingdom will not start till after his death (i, 259–65). He cunningly allows Satan to remain in ignorance of this crucial fact throughout the poem, thus wrecking his whole temptation-strategy, which is based on a normal expectation of life. Satan's frantic (and perfectly accurate) examination of Christ's horoscope discloses only the 'violence' and 'cruel death' that Christ already knows about. His anxious assurances that he can find no news of a kingdom there are quite sincere but, for Christ, quite unworrying (iv, 381–93). Exactly how his kingdom will come about, Christ does not know ('Even the Son', wrote Milton in *Christian Doctrine*, citing *Mark* xiii, 32 and *Matthew* xxiv, 36, 'knows not all things absolutely; there being some secret purposes, the knowledge of which the Father has reserved to himself alone'). He ingeniously conceals this deficiency from Satan without actually lying: 'Means there shall be to this, but what the means,/Is not for thee to know, nor me to tell' (iv, 152–3).

Christ's unnerving certainty about the future of the sooth-saying profession ('henceforth Oracles are ceast', i, 456) sounds as if it must be supernatural, until we notice that anyone who had read *Micah* v (from which Milton quotes when discussing astrology in *Christian Doctrine*) could make the same deduction: 'But thou, Bethlehem Ephratah, . . . out of thee shall he come forth unto me that is to be ruler in Israel. . . . And it shall come to pass in that day, saith the Lord, that I will cut off . . . witchcrafts out of thine hand; and thou shalt have no more soothsayers.'

It certainly crosses Satan's mind that the character he is up against is superhuman. He tells the devils that he is 'With more than human gifts from Heav'n adorn'd' (ii, 37). Before he takes

Christ up to the pinnacle, though, he tells him that so far as he can see he is just a man (iv, 535–6). No doubt he has reason for lying on both occasions, but unless we assume that he is still in genuine doubt, it is not clear how we can explain what happens when they get to the pinnacle. This is the hardest question about *Paradise Regained*. The right answer, as we shall see, is not fully available, but several wrong ones can be discounted.

Biblical commentators disagreed about what the 'pinnacle' (the word used in *Matthew* iv, 5 and *Luke* iv, 9) was like. Some said it was a flat roof, on which Christ could easily stand upright; others, that it was a peaked gable or spire (a nearby word in Milton's description, iv, 548). These explained Christ's ability to stay on it by saying there was just enough room, or that Satan held him. One at least, Thomas Bilson (1547–1616), suggested it was a miracle. But if Christ did a miracle to stop himself falling, it would mean he distrusted God just as surely as if he had done a miracle to stop himself starving. We must relinquish this, then, as the major commentators did. But on the other hand Milton's pinnacle is so small that Satan expects Christ to fall off, as Milton is careful to tell us (iv, 571). Satan's sarcasm shows this, too: 'to stand upright/Will ask thee skill' (iv, 551–2). Crouching terror and a dizzy plunge are what he looks for. Maybe the angelic rescue team will turn out, maybe not. Either way Satan will have solved his problem, with a divine Christ or a dead one. But Christ just stands there. If it is a miracle, and not Christ's, it must be the Father's. But we are turned back from this way out too. The angels get there in time, Milton says, to whisk Christ away from his 'uneasy station' (iv, 583–4). Standing, then, was difficult, so miraculous aid must be ruled out. What we are left with is a balancing feat—an astonishing one, certainly. Josephus, the 1st-century Jewish historian, whose work Milton knew well, had written of the temple portico overlooking the Kedron ravine:

> The valley was very deep, and its bottom could not be seen if you looked from above into the depth. The high elevation of the portico stood upon that height, that if anyone looked down from the top of the roof to those depths, he would be giddy, while his sight could not reach down to such an abyss.  ANTIQUITIES XV, xi, 5

Christ has a steeplejack's nerve as well as a detective's brain. It is the ending we should expect after watching his icy calm during interrogation. Satan is 'smitten with amazement' (iv, 562), though, and loses his footing. That, at least, is our first impression, but Satan, we discover, is also struck with 'anguish' and 'dread' (iv, 576). Presumably 'anguish . . . To find himself not matchless', as in *Paradise Lost* vi, 340, but why dread? We get no help from the gospels, where Satan does not even fall, but just goes away. Does his 'dread' mean he at last recognises his companion? The way the word has been used previously, suggests it may. We recall: 'thy Father's ire,/(Whose ire I dread more than the fire of Hell)' (iii, 219-20). What he then took to be a 'meek regard' which might provide a 'shelter' from God's ire (iii, 217-21), is, he may now realise, just a relaxed form of the horrible face Christ pulled (a 'count'nance too severe to be beheld') to scare him into jumping from Heaven's battlements. The 'severe' face, which represented God's 'ire' , and made Satan jump to find a 'shelter' from it (*PL* vi, 824-64), and this meek one are, it may now disconcertingly strike him, the same. He is sheltering in a bomb-store. The simile of the sphinx who 'Cast herself headlong from th'Ismenian steep' (iv, 575) indicates that Satan does not fall, but jumps, terrified to find who he is out on a limb with. Maybe it is Christ's reply that enlightens him: 'Also it is written,/Tempt not the Lord thy God' (iv, 560-1). Orthodox (Christ is quoting *Deuteronomy* vi, 16), authentic (it is what Christ says in *Luke* iv, 12), this reply means on the surface 'I will not cast myself down, because that would be to make trial of God, which Deuteronomy forbids'. But it could mean 'I am the Lord thy God, do not tempt me'. Some early commentators, chiefly Church Fathers, thought this was what Christ intended, but most theologians in Milton's day were against the idea. Giving way to Satan's pressure, and claiming divinity, would not fit in with Christ's previous policy of mystification. Satan, though, may misunderstand, and leap in terror from a quite harmless biblical text. And Christ (we simply cannot be sure) may reckon on Satan's misunderstanding. He picks a dummy missile which, given his opponent's nervous condition, is bound to be mistaken for the real thing.

But from beginning to end Christ does not lay a finger on Satan, or do any magic, or tell an untruth. He lives by his wits.

THE TEMPTATIONS

Milton, unlike most Renaissance artists, took the order of his temptations (stones-into-bread; kingdoms-of-the-world; pinnacle) from *Luke* iv, 1–13 rather than *Matthew* iv, 1–11 which reverses the second and third. He did this so as to leave the pinnacle and Satanic high-dive for his climax. He also inserted an unbiblical banquet between the first two, and an unbiblical storm between the last two, and split off Athens from the other kingdoms to make it a separate temptation: knowledge.

Strictly, though, there are no temptations in *Paradise Regained*, only rejections. Satan, like the author of *Paradise Lost*, makes the most of the attractions of opulence and conquest. But what is now being put over is the low mental age to which they appeal. Christ, with all the responsiveness of 'solid rock' (iv, 18), sterilises the poem's core, while Satan prowls impotently round him. Like any Jewish toddler, Christ had dreamed of beating the bad Romans and being 'admir'd by all' (i, 214–17), and, though willing to try persuasion first, had seen no contradiction in stopping 'Brute violence' by force (i, 219–26). But these were growing pains, and when he talked to his mother about them she told him that his career was to be cut to a more unusual pattern (i, 227–33). Of Milton's two dreams, Christ, when the poem opens, has chosen that of the hermit (i, 8).

Satan starts on the wrong foot by expecting Christ to want power—it is the only ambition he can imagine (i, 98–9). This puts him at a disadvantage throughout. Not that the world-power he has to offer amounts, when he thinks about it, to much. After all, he was an angel once, so naturally has bigger ideas. For the first three-and-a-half books he seems, when trying to corrupt Christ, as small-minded as any field-marshal, and even when he is at home with the devils his heroes are Scipio Africanus and Alexander the Great (i, 196–200)—at least, he thinks their line of country 'manlier' than the pursuit of beauty (ii, 195–225), a

Satanism confidently ascribed to Milton himself by some readers. But he sees through 'honour, glory and popular praise' from the start (i, 227–8, compare iii, 25–8), and later, in conversation with Christ, brushes aside 'the Kingdoms of this world' (iv, 210), as if he well knows what trash he has been marketing. Still, power, as an idea, has irresistible attraction for him (the disciples also think of Christ as a power-figure (ii, 36, 48): revenge and nationalism are what they want). Eventually Satan offers even knowledge in terms of power, peddling Aristotle as the man 'who bred/Great Alexander to subdue the world' (iv, 251–2), music as the 'secret power' of harmony (iv, 254–5), oratory as 'resistless eloquence'—how to make enemies and influence people.

Whereas Christ listens searchingly to Satan (so piercing his disguise straight off), Satan, whether through egotism, frayed nerves, or lack of imagination, is unable to keep his mind on what his companion says. After the banquet, for instance, Christ has a speech which ought to alter the whole course of the poem (ii, 433–86), because it explains that he knows everything worth knowing (ii, 443–4), and that no 'generous mind' would want to rule anyone by force (ii, 479–80). If Satan were listening he would see that the ammunition he laboriously expends in the next two books—the 'temptations' of Parthia, Rome and Athens—is already obsolete.

Christ uses his intelligence aggressively, as well as for self-defence. He muddles his floundering opponent. Though his speech after the banquet has its straightforward (and so revealing) moments, Christ lays false trails at the same time by pretending to admire the 'mighty things' accomplished by a selection of Roman fighting-men (ii, 446–8), and asking innocently whether he may not 'as soon/Accomplish what they did, perhaps and more' (ii, 451–2). It sounds as if he is planning to fight, though privately he means 'different in kind' by 'more'. 'What if with like aversion I reject/Riches and Realms?' (ii, 457–8), is teasingly noncommittal, and so is Christ's conclusion that sceptres are 'oftest better miss't' (ii, 486), because it leaves Satan to discover whether there are some which are better caught. The mixture of false-trail and honesty makes this speech of Christ's as self-contradictory as Satan's when he was pretending to be a rustic, but Christ is sharp enough to seize inconsistencies and Satan is not. Christ continues his war of nerves in the second half. After the Rome panorama he condescends to touch up Satan's temptation with some additional luxuries, before knocking it down (iv, 113–21). Satan is bound to wonder how he knows so much about Roman depravity, and so Christ dangles the source of his knowledge (actually his precocious bookishness, see i, 201–3) just out of Satan's reach: 'For I also have heard, perhaps have read' (iv, 116). He flexes his muscles jocularly while chatting about Tiberius—'I shall, thou say'st, expel/A brutish monster; what if I withal/Expel a Devil who first made him such?' (iv, 127–9), enjoying, we take it, Satan's apprehensive look.

Even Satan's cunning seems over-anxious, and gets in its own way. The banquet tries to do too many things at once. Satan assures the devils it will contain 'that which only seems to satisfy/Lawful desires of Nature, not beyond' (ii, 229–30), but its opulence and its paederasts (ii, 352–3—perhaps a last-minute brainwave of whichever devil was doing the stage-management) are out of key with this. The chivalric aspects of the cuisine (ii, 360–1) look as if Satan is trying to include the attractions of 'honour' and 'glory', which he had mentioned to the devils as alternatives to plain cooking (ii, 227). Satan took a lofty tone with Belial when he suggested they might leave women about where Christ would see them (ii, 153–224)—'None are, thou think'st, but taken with such toys'. (We gather he treats women as toys because of his inability to love. He pathetically corrects himself when discussing the matter with Christ (i, 379–80)—'I have not lost/To love, at least contemplate and admire'). But women do figure in the banquet-temptation (ii, 355–7). Further, though Satan tells Christ twice that the banquet does not contain 'Meats by the Law unclean' (ii, 328, 369–70), it does (shellfish: see *Deuteronomy* xiv, 9–10). Either Satan has slipped up, or the inconsistencies are intentional. He expects Christ to opt out of the banquet and then have to explain why he has not a right to shellfish and girls along with the rest of created things, if he is the Son of God (ii, 324).

But this means that the original idea of the banquet as temptation has outgrown itself, and now it is having to be attractive and repulsive at once. Christ, in reply, refuses to be pinned down about his universal rights, but pretends, exasperatingly, to take Satan's word for them: 'Said'st thou not that to all things I had right?/And who witholds my pow'r that right to use?' (ii, 379–80).

This quick-mindedness unsettles Satan, and his indecision worsens. His most emotional speech (iii, 204–22) changes direction half way through, disowning hope and fear—'For where no hope is left, is left no fear' (iii, 206), then claiming both urgently—'to that gentle brow/Willingly I could fly, and hope thy reign . . . Would stand between me and thy Father's ire,/(Whose ire I dread more than the fire of Hell)' (iii, 215–20). Milton leaves us to estimate what has happened inside Satan as best we can. At least we are told he really is 'inly rackt' at the start, so the hopelessness is genuine. Caught off his guard, Satan lets drop for a moment the mask which shields him from his despair (as he did on Niphates, *PL* iv, 32–113). But his pride rebels at the exhibition he is making of himself, and he tries to turn it (in the middle of iii, 215) into an appeal to Christ's better feelings. Then, as his confidence flows back, even tempting Christ to pity seems beneath him, and he transfers briskly to another argument—'If I then to the worst that can be haste' (iii, 223)—without giving Christ a chance to pity him after all. We are left to imagine the cool disbelief on Christ's face. Milton tactfully lets the dramatic transitions speak for themselves.

Satan finds difficulty in making his words come out straight. His hatred keeps blurting out from behind the hypocrisy. 'What can be then less in me than desire/To see thee and approach thee?' (i, 383–4), says the opposite of what it means to. Presenting the banquet—'behold/Nature asham'd, or better to express,/Troubl'd' (ii, 331–3)—he catches himself just in time. 'That thou mayst know I seek not to engage/Thy Virtue, and not every way secure/On no slight grounds thy safety . . .' (iii, 347–9) shows him tussling with his negatives to stop them giving him away. When he asks Christ to fall down and worship him—

'For what can less so great a gift deserve?' (iv, 169)—we recognise his old impediment.

'Fall down,/And worship me' is a price-tag added after Christ has expressed lack of interest in what Satan has to offer (iv, 110–53). The illogicality of the sales-technique exposes it as a fake: a clumsy attempt to prod Christ into a heated assertion of his own status (theologians had commonly read Satan's demand in this way). Christ contemplates the ulterior motive with 'disdain', and uninformatively quotes the Bible (iv, 175–7).

The knowledge-temptation (iv, 236–84) shows how seriously Satan has been affected by the constant reverses. It is by far the worst managed. The power-obsession that stands out all over it merely tells us that Satan's character is getting the better of his intelligence, but he seems to have taken leave of his senses when he advances pagan fables ('Phoebus' envying Homer's poems, iv, 260) and the glorification of 'fate, and chance' (iv, 265) as if they could cut any ice with a man of Christ's opinions. Quoting an oracle's attribution of supreme wisdom (iv, 275–6) to a pagan philosopher whom Christ has already relegated beneath Job (iii, 96), is particularly obtuse in view of Christ's denunciation of oracles (i, 430–64). These gaffes may seem to be unfairly planted by Milton, rather than issuing from Satan's personality, but their purpose is clearly to convey that he is almost out of his mind with worry.

The ugly dreams and supernatural storm which Satan arranges next (iv, 408–26) are often read as a temptation to distrust (like stones-into-bread). Certainly Satan seems to want to make Christ believe that the atmospherics constitute an evil omen in which he himself has no hand (iv, 465–82). Just before the storm, though, Milton says that Satan is 'Quite at a loss, for all his darts were spent' (iv, 366), and he approaches Christ with his suggestion about omens, we are told, 'with no new device, they all were spent,/Rather by this his last affront resolv'd/Desperate of better course, to vent his rage/And mad despite to be so oft repell'd' (iv, 443–6). The double stage-direction insists that what may seem a new plan is mere spite. Christ himself reads more purpose into Satan's behaviour than Milton's instructions will allow, when he accuses Satan of 'thinking to terrify/Mee to thy will' (iv, 496–7). Perhaps pure spite is inconceivable to so rational a being. At all events, Christ gives the devil more than his due when he credits him with a policy of intimidation. However Satan may pretend to himself or Christ that he is still carrying out some policy at this stage, impotent fury, Milton tells us, is what seethes beneath his smooth talk about the weather (iv, 451–83). The information that the storm is an 'affront' not a 'device' proves that Satan's condition has deteriorated since the start of Book iv. Even then, before the montage of Rome and Athens, Milton is prepared to tell us (it comes as a surprise) that Satan has abandoned any hope of success (iv, 23). He keeps tempting partly, as later, for 'spite', but partly to salvage his reputation (iv, 12). Somewhere between this juncture and the storm, even the image of himself as a respectable loser has faded.

Christ has two weak moments. The first concerns glory. His denunciation (Senecan not Christian) of the 'rabble', disposes of glory unequivocally (iii, 47–56). 'True glory', Christ explains, comes from God; 'false glory' from men (iii, 60–9). He starts to shuffle out of this corner even before the end of his speech. 'If there be in glory aught of good' (iii, 88), is a concession he cannot now afford; and he talks about Socrates' fame among men as if it were distinctly desirable (iii, 99). Satan sees his chance, and quietly moves in, 'murmuring' (iii, 108) that God 'requires/Glory from men, from all men good or bad' (iii, 113–14). It is a deadly blow, and has Christ staggering, hot with anger (iii, 121), logic scattered to the winds. 'And reason; since his word all things produc'd' (iii, 122) is a wild rejoinder. The question is why God should *want* glory from the 'rabble', by whom, so Christ said, 'to be disprais'd were no small praise' (iii, 56). All the answers he now tries—that God made the rabble in the first place; that self-glorification was not actually all he had in mind; that men ought to glorify him anyway—fall desperately wide of the mark. The champion is in real trouble. But Milton calmly puts an end to the round: 'Satan had not to answer' (iii, 146). We cannot believe it. The poem, which had seemed so tightly argued, suddenly looks a put-up job. We see that it has no way of squaring Christ's Stoicism with his glory-hungry God, and we may be led to suspect, once the crack has opened, that his pacifism—'They err who count it glorious to subdue/By Conquest' (iii, 71–2)—would not appeal, either, to the Jehovah whose germ-warfare (70,000 dead in three days) Christ coolly blames Satan for provoking (iii, 409–12).

Christ's second lapse is his rejection of Greek poetry. 'I once had a pupil,' C. S. Lewis recalls, 'innocent alike of the Greek and of the Hebrew tongue, who did not think himself thereby disqualified from pronouncing this judgment a proof of Milton's bad taste.' And he adds: 'The unpopular passage is better understood if we remember that it reflects a literary opinion which Milton had, in some form or other, held all his life.' The point is not, though, whether Christ's comparative-literature is up to scratch, or whether it can be excused as a permanent aberration of Milton's. The weakness of Christ's onslaught on the shameless Greeks (iv, 342) resides in its excitement, not its provincialism. To detect this, one tongue is sufficient.

> Remove their swelling Epithets thick laid
> As varnish on a Harlot's cheek, the rest,
> Thin sown with aught of profit or delight,
> Will far be found unworthy to compare
> With Sion's songs, to all true tastes excelling,
> Where God is prais'd aright.

iv, 343–7

Whatever has happened to our impassive hero? His grammar, we notice, falls over itself. To say that, if the epithets are removed, 'the rest' will be short of profit or delight is to imply that profit and delight might be found in the epithets, a notion which the speaker's testiness about cosmetics (originally Claudius's in *Hamlet* III, i, 53) works decisively against. If the epithets are themselves such an eyesore why must they be removed before Greek poetry can be found 'unworthy to compare/With Sion's songs'?

Christ's shrillness here is less damaging than his first mistake, of course, and may even be a part of Milton's planning. It is a good build-up for the climax that the rock should seem less solid than usual, and anti-Hellenic fanaticism would be historically likely in a Jew who could see the results of the gradual Hellenisation of Judaea since 167 B.C. when Antiochus had violated the Holy of Holies. Even the blunder about glory, though a doctrinal mishap, might be valued for its moment of drama.

The poem has a deeper inadequacy. A much-signposted element of its structure (and a theological cliché) is Christ's status as an improved edition of Adam-and-Eve (see i, 1–4; ii, 154–5, 348–9; iv, 180). The pros and cons of the comparison are ingeniously multiplied: Christ in a 'pathless desert' (i, 296), Eve in a garden; his solitude better than 'choicest society' (i, 302), hers making her a 'stray Ewe' (i, 315); both surrounded by tame animals (i, 310), both having Satanic dreams (iv, 408); Satan approaching both 'girded with snaky wiles' (i, 120). The unscriptural knowledge-temptation (Athens) extends the parallel. We are persuaded that Christ would have done better than Eve. But better than Adam? The celibate detective is never imagined in a domestic crisis like Adam's, and however willing we are to believe that he would have handled it faultlessly, we must notice that the poem only skirts the problem of showing us just how he would have found a way of deserting his wife. Satan has the air of a character brushing something aside for his author when he approaches the question: 'Adam by his Wife's allurement fell,/However to this Man inferior far' (ii, 134–5). Besides, he seems to be wrong, since Christ is merely 'perfect Man' (i, 166) as Adam was (*PL* v, 524). The women Belial suggests tempting Christ with seem intended as recollections of Eve—at least, he uses words which have been used about her: 'like to Goddesses' (ii, 156, see *PL* v, 380–2); 'graceful and discreet' (ii, 157, see *PL* viii, 550, 600); 'Virgin majesty' (ii, 159, *PL* ix, 270)— but the correspondence is shallow, and only emphasises the comparative complexity of Adam's choice. Christ's ordeal fails to match Adam's, with the result that the claims *Paradise Regained* makes for parity cannot be met, and its version of life, though tense, is easier. Adam has to reckon with emotional involvements to which balancing on a steeple would be no answer.

# 9

# The Outmoded Hero: Samson

*Samson Agonistes* (the second word could mean 'spiritual struggler' or just 'athlete') may have been finished in the 1650s, but came out in the same volume as *Paradise Regained* (1671), and its hero serves as a barbaric foil to the new Christian hero of that poem. Theologians had pretended that the biblical Samson was a foreshadowing of Christ: Milton uses him as contrast. The Jewish characters make much of Samson's renunciation of 'proud Arms' (137), but it is a quibble merely. Samson is 'Himself an Army' (346). Christ's disarmament (*PR* iii, 400–1) has moral significance; Samson's, none. The play's 'good' figures place a solemn emphasis on the glory of a good physique, fame, conquest, and other discarded values. Christ's contempt for 'war' and 'violence' which destroy 'the flourishing works of peace' (*PR* iii, 80–91) might make any reader think about Samson's theatre-demolition. Samson believes that killing people (his previous occupation) was 'indeed heroic' (527), but the chorus, though hardly qualified to disabuse him (see 125–38), are made to insert Milton's opinion when they point out that 'the wise' count 'Patience as the truest fortitude' (654) (compare 'the better fortitude/Of patience', *PL* ix, 31–2). 'Patience' was essential to Christ's heroism in *Paradise Regained* (see ii, 432; iii, 92–3; iv, 420). The play wants to purge its audience of passion (1758) but exhibits a figure who escapes it only in death.

## SAMSON'S PSYCHE
Milton takes a brutal old romance, with vestiges of solar myth (Samson, the sun, 'shorn of his beams' by winter or the sea) and turns it into a psychological drama by inventing confrontations

(Samson with himself, with the chorus, with Manoa, with Dalila, with Harapha) in each of which a passionate egotist finds a new way of coping with his rage and resentment. The Greek tragic form (a string of episodes, each with two speakers only, each sealed off from the next by choric recitation, all violence taking place off stage), provides laboratory conditions for observing Samson's inner shifts.

Samson is generally said to undergo gradual 'regeneration', first blaming God, then himself, then regaining self-respect in opposing Dalila, and so being able to defy Harapha. There seems, though, no spiritual development, only a change of circumstances which eventually allows the resentment, which has been gnawing inwardly, to hit out. It is difficult to believe that Samson would have reacted less violently to Harapha's taunts had they come at the start. He is quick enough, early on, to defend himself against the mild reproof of the chorus (219–26, 241–76).

Before the chorus enter it has disturbingly occurred to him that what has happened may be his fault (44–6), but he suppresses the idea, blaming instead a faulty mixture of strength and wisdom in his design (53–64) and the nuisance of needing eyes to see with (93–7). So long as he cannot be overheard, he steeps himself in self-pity (his most moving occupation: nothing else approaches this first speech in emotional power), switching easily between questioning God's management and telling himself not to (43–4, 60–1). We are conscious, once the chorus enter, of a change in Samson's emphasis. He begins to think of the impression he is making. 'O loss of sight, of thee I most complain' (67), gives way to the more histrionic 'Yet that which was the worst now least afflicts me,/Blindness, for had I sight, confus'd with shame,/ How could I once look up?' (195–7). His self-contempt ('Fool, have divulg'd the secret gift of God', 201) is a channel for his resentment, but also a defence against criticism, and a screen for self-pity. The resentment is still glad of other targets—imagined slanderers (202–5), or God's workmanship (205–9). Significantly he combines his orgy of self-criticism ('She was not the prime cause, but I myself', 234) with heated excuses whenever his friends try to join in ('what I motion'd was of God', 222; 'That fault I take not on me', 241). Something less pure than humility underlies his new eagerness to shoulder blame. Fittingly the episode ends with lines that set the grandiose—'Of such examples add mee to the roll'—beside the self-deprecatory—'Mee easily indeed mine may neglect' (290-1).

Even the chorus notice some exaggeration in Samson's behaviour— 'Deject not then so overmuch thyself' (213)—and Manoa diagnoses his son's 'self-rigorous' extremes as a sign that he is 'self-displeas'd/For self-offence, more than for God offended' (513-15). In the interview with Dalila his pride in being 'self-severe' (827) is unconcealed. The final 'self-violence' (1584) rounds off an almost unwavering self-absorption on Samson's part, which makes the chorus's confidence that self-love is a womanly failing (1031) rebound upon them ludicrously.

The episode with Manoa starts well for Samson's ego, since he has the satisfaction of off-loading the chorus's reprimand ('Tax not divine disposal', 210) on to his father (373). He continues to mix denunciations and excuses with assurances that it was all his own fault. He turns Dalila improbably into a besieging army, with 'assaults' and 'batteries' (404-6), and complains that she kept him awake, but forestalls criticism by pouring insults on his own conduct ('foul effeminacy', not 'a grain of manhood', 408-10), even confessing that he knew all along (as the Samson of *Judges* must have guessed) that Dalila was going to betray him (397-9). His vigorous admission that he has got his deserts (412-13), and his highmindedness about his 'former servitude'— worse, so he says, than blindness (418)—sound affectedly noble when we glance back at the private agony: 'Inferior to the vilest now become/Of man or worm; the vilest here excel me,/They creep, yet see' (74-5). It would be hugely insensitive to suggest that Samson is putting on an act. The pressure behind his language precludes anything so calculated. But the nature of his audience is forcing him, as he sees it, to turn against himself indignation which he desperately wants to divert elsewhere— hence the undercurrent of excuse, and the hint of attitudinising.

Determined as he is that no one will be harder on him than he is himself, it must be an unsettling moment when Manoa opens a new aspect of the affair by asserting that God is being 'Dis-glorified', and that Samson should think this the heaviest of his sufferings (433–7). Samson tackles this new humble pie manfully, making out the damage to be even more shocking than Manoa appreciates (448–56), and claiming it as his 'chief affliction'—the very thing that has been keeping him awake at night (457–9). So far as we can see, though, it has not occurred to him before. His own shame and suffering, not God's, have occupied his attention, and he is, it transpires, unwilling to have the centre of interest shifted. Once he has collected his wits, he points out to Manoa that God's case is not so bad after all, since he is bound to win, and quickly (460–71). Samson then returns to belabouring himself (487–501), and soon forgets about how God will get on without him: 'This only hope relieves me' (460) is effaced by 'Nor am I in the list of them that hope' (647).

'Pride', Samson gives out he can see, was the cause of his downfall (532). But that his resolution to stay in prison, and his instant equation of an 'obscure' life in his father's house with a 'contemptible' one (572), are the same pride, is beyond his moral perception. Manoa reasonably argues that by working in the mill he is helping his and God's enemies (577–8), but Samson is too self-absorbed to imagine how his ordeal affects anyone but himself. It was a new idea of Milton's to have Manoa sue with the Philistines for the release of his son. What he gains is a demonstration of Samson's perversity. For all his complaints about conditions at the mill, he would not be without them for a moment. He refuses to hear of his sight being restored, when Manoa brightly suggests it (590–8). With Samson, being filthy and 'Put to the labour of a beast' is, Milton takes steps to assure us, a matter of choice. He will not be cheated of his torment. At the mill he can at least be violent against someone, if only himself. Obduracy of this common kind could hardly be called spiritual progress, and when Samson, after the first two episodes, gives a review of his position, we see that no advance has been made. Though he told his father not to 'appoint' (arraign) heavenly disposition, he is still aggrieved that God should have let him down: 'He . . . hath cast me off as never known,/And to those cruel enemies,/Whom I by his appointment had provok't,/Left me all helpless' (641-4). Samson is having nothing more educative than a tragic sulk.

Being an index of rage, not humility, Samson's self-condemnation can soon turn to attack if a suitable object appears. If 'She was not the prime cause, but I myself' (234) had come from any depth, it could not so easily be replaced by 'Out, out Hyaena!' (748) the moment Dalila walks in.

The motive behind Dalila's treachery, and her return (a Miltonic invention), is obscure. Like her husband, she makes excuses while insisting that she is 'without excuse' (734), and at first these are plainly lies. She tries to pass the betrayal off as inquisitiveness and girlish chatter (774-7), but soon reveals that it was premeditated. Her claim to religious and political loyalties is ventured, one suspects, mainly for its Samson-appeal. Later, when promising herself a national memorial, she hints that her patriotism—'the piety/Which to my country I was judg'd to have shown' (993-4)—will be in the eye of the beholder. The motive Samson suggests—money (830-1)—is brutally simple but probably nearer the truth: presumably Dalila's luxurious equipage (712-22) is meant to bear it out. But the motive that best fits with her attempt to get Samson back is possessiveness (790-812). Dalila implies she did not guess the Philistines would blind Samson (736-7, 800-2). There seems no cause to question this. After all, Samson knew she was going to betray him (397-9), so could not conceivably have forecast the actual result either. From what we see of Dalila, she would not have wanted her husband disfigured. If she thought 'safe custody' (802) all the Philistines intended, and that she could talk Samson round afterwards (881), her treachery was quite reasonable. His physique made him necessary to her sexual appetite, and naturally she did not want him wasted in battle (804). Samson knows how 'furious' her physical demands are, and ungallantly rephrases but does not dispute this motive when she frankly offers it (836-7). After Samson, other men are likely to leave Dalila with a feeling of insufficiency, and it is put to us that an emptiness in her bed (806) has goaded this delicate creature to come and plead in publi : with a slave. Hopefully she reminds him that 'other senses want not their delights' (916).

Samson avoids, rather than resists, her temptation. Terrified of feeling her body against his, he warns her to keep her distance (ostensibly for her own safety—but why should this concern him?) (725, 951–3). At first he uses her as a handy receptacle for rage, flinging accusations which include the wildly improbable (that she has come back just for 'malice', 821) and the distinctly untrue (that he was deceived, 750). His façade of argument will not stand up to much probing. We have heard him say that he married a Philistine because he thought it would give him a better chance to 'oppress' her nation (232–3). Now that he needs something to throw at Dalila he maintains he married her for love, and makes a virtue of having chosen her 'before all the daughters of my Tribe' (876–9). One or both of these accounts must be less than completely truthful, and the first puts him in an impossible position to accuse Dalila of mixing patriotism with marriage (885–6). His casuistry about gods who sanction 'ungodly deeds' not being real gods (896–900)—curiously reminiscent of what Satan said to Eve, *PL* ix, 700–1—is question-begging at best. Milton (it is characteristic of him not to avoid the difficulty) allows Dalila the retort that the Hebrew God approves of driving nails into guests' heads (987–90). When Samson's first fury has blown over he is audibly moved by the gentleness of Dalila's offer: 'No, no, of my condition take no care;/It fits not' (928–9) is an unmistakable tone-change. There is not even (as when Manoa made his offer) a pretence of high motive in Samson's refusal to leave the mill now. Having temporarily expended his anger, he does not need to stay, and mere self-interest decides him. Blindness, he reckons, will put him at a disadvantage with Dalila, and if she tires of him he will be neglected (941–4). He does not see himself as overcoming a temptation, but as being warily selfish.

When Dalila has gone Samson still harbours his morose conviction that God is being spiteful—'God sent her to debase me,/And aggravate my folly' (999–1000)—and still protests hastily that of course he deserves it—'who committed/To such a viper his most sacred trust' (1000–1). The double-talk is by this time familiar.

The next visitor produces a different reaction not because Samson has been 'ennobled' but because Harapha, unlike God or Dalila, both arouses resentment and provides it with an uncomplicated outlet. It is no doubt encouraging to Samson, too, to discover that he can still terrify. We are unlikely to be persuaded that the episode shows him in any real sense Harapha's moral superior, since he finds self-fulfilment, as Harapha habitually does, in bombast and violence. Nor does he make out a better case than Harapha, whose accusations of murder and robbery are just (1185–8; *Judges* xiv, 19). All Samson's reply amounts to is that it seemed reasonable to him to kill thirty innocent men because thirty quite different men had outwitted him (1201–4). What can be deduced from the encounter is that the simple task of hating someone so occupies Samson that his own condition presses upon him less. God's justice and pardon and his own error can now be taken very much for granted (1170–4), while Samson's attention is given to defiance. His 'spiritual recovery' is a relapse—a return to a less reflective state. The change effected by this encounter can be exaggerated too. Samson pulls himself together at the chance of a brawl, and so finds himself feeling God is on his side again (1357), but he does not, any more than before, want to go on living (1262–3). We are shown that the blindness which tore those desolate cries from him at the start has, beneath the arguments and posturing, weighed more heavily with him all along, and still does, than any new chance of serving God. He is not one of the patient souls the chorus tell him about (1287–96).

Given Samson's truculence with Harapha, his dismissal of the Philistine officer is what we should expect. When, moments later, he changes his mind, we should be unconvinced if Milton did not plainly indicate that Samson is now in receipt of premonitions from God. These start to filter through even before the officer arrives, when Samson first has the idea that those who kill him may 'Draw their own ruin' (1267), and they recur with increasing clarity (1347, 1377–9), though he has not yet understood, even when his exit comes, quite what is afoot (1388-9, 1427). Because Samson does not go off under his own steam, psychologically speaking, the play may be said to insist at this turning-point of its action (the point called in Greek theory the *peripeteia*) that it is not a drama of inner regeneration. With this old type of hero (unlike the new model hero of *Paradise Regained*) God still has to pull the strings.

What looks like a planned contrast in the 1671 volume between the New Testament Christ and the Old Testament Samson helps one to believe that criticism of the Israelites might have been a part of Milton's design in his lurid finale. Manoa is given a speech praising the 'magnanimity' of the Philistine lords who agree to forgo revenge, and distinguishing them from the religious fanatics, 'Contemptuous, proud, set on revenge and spite' (1462-71). This is an odd preparation for the news of Samson's revenge, and for Manoa's grisly elation at the size of the disaster (1711-12). We notice, also, that Milton positions Manoa's 'joy' at the idea of 'heaps of slaughtered' (1531-2) immediately before the entrance of the frantic messenger running away from the sickening fact (1543). Though he does not realise it Manoa plans a tomb and floral tributes for Samson which clearly match those Dalila promised herself (986-7, 1733-42). There is less to choose between them, we might infer, than a tribal enthusiast would like to think. (Samson's regret that he has strength without wisdom links him with the chorus's opinion of Dalila—'outward ornament' but 'judgment scant', 1025-7.)

Of course, the closing scenes contain religious orthodoxy as well: we must not over-press the ironies. The most we may grant is that Milton has done less than he might to stop us reading the play's ending as a celebration of savagery, and *Samson Agonistes* is a better work because, by placing Manoa and his cronies in this doubtful light, it has gone some way towards surmounting the crudity of its climax.

If the play has a major limitation it is not to be found here but in the thinness of its characterisation. As we have seen, Samson's inner life consists of resentment, self-pity and hatred: intense, but negative. The other figures—Manoa, Dalila, Harapha—have being as roles and arguments, not characters. We hear their evidence and assign motives, but cannot approach nearer. The most impoverishing result is that we come up against a blank at the play's centre when we try to imagine the relationship between Dalila and Samson. Samson hardly seems sure of it himself. Although (in Milton, not the Bible) Dalila is his wife, he calls her his 'concubine' (537)—'a woman who cohabits with a man without being his wife', says the OED firmly. When we catch him borrowing Othello's words (878–81) we feel the incongruity of it. Milton makes him a chaster figure than the biblical Samson, who frequented brothels (*Judges* xvi, 1). This Samson calls his wife 'lascivious' (536), and his Nazarite vow is spoken of as if it entailed celibacy ('strictest purity', 319), which it did not (see *Numbers* vi, 1–21). When we hear of him chopping down 'a thousand foreskins' with his 'sword of bone' (143–4) we suspect that Milton is converting him into a vehicle for his own sterile loathings. So, too, when Samson becomes a 'self-begotten' phoenix (1699) rising from its 'ashy womb' (the blighted fruition reflects in other nouns and adjectives, 'fatal harvest', 1024, for instance, and 'mortal seed', 1439). This Puritan Samson naturally gets in the way when we try to picture him as Dalila's husband. The chorus, too, make it harder to keep a steady image of his personality by paying him inept compliments—pretending that he overcomes 'feats of war' with 'plain heroic magnitude of mind' (1278–9), or including 'wit' among his accomplishments (1010). The play is acted out by figures who possess colour and energy, but not depth.

# 10

# End Note

Milton's poetry is about, to put it barely, Good Conduct. This is why a study of how he uses words makes him look more of a poet than a study of what he uses them for. But we miss his true stature if we reduce him to a stylist. He is, massively, a moral phenomenon. The less palatable implications of this are no more to be explained away than the encouraging ones.

Preoccupied with Sage and Hero, he had nothing but contempt for the common man: the contempt that nourishes idealism or atrocity. He had no ability to store the popular imagination with folk heroes as Shakespeare or Dickens can. He apprehends people as theories. Morality to him means repression, not relationship. He is repelled by organic life: in his dream his wife returns 'washt from spot of childbed taint'. He never really imagines how evil might be turned into good. He wants it isolated, locked away, exterminated.

Against this we must put his fearless reappraisal of religious and social orthodoxies. His alertness to the Satanic self-importance behind political and military leadership. His growing disillusionment with violence. His insistence on the responsibilities entailed in being alive: the need for unrelaxed reason and individual choice. His refusal, finally, to ignore the awkward and the challenging. It is when his morality is furthest from the contentedly diagrammatic that he produces his greatest poem, *Paradise Lost*, pitting a ruined Hero against a travesty of the Sage, and showing Man making a passionate choice which we will not let our reason condemn.

# Further Reading

## WORKS

*The Works of John Milton*, ed. F. A. Patterson (Columbia Univ. Press, New York, 1940).
*Complete Prose Works* (Yale Univ. Press, New Haven, Conn., 1953-9).
*John Milton, Complete Poems and Major Prose*, ed. M. Y. Hughes Odyssey Press, New York, 1958).

## BIOGRAPHY

*The Early Lives of Milton*, ed. Helen Darbishire (Barnes & Noble, New York, 1965).
Johnson, S., *Lives of the English Poets* (Oxford Univ. Press, New York).
*The Life Records of John Milton*, ed. J. M. French (Rutgers Univ. Press, New Brunswick, N.J., 1968).

## CRITICISM

Tuve, Rosemond, *Images and Themes in Five Poems by Milton* (Harvard Univ. Press, Cambridge, Mass., 1957).
*Milton: A Collection of Critical Essays*, ed. L. L. Martz (Prentice-Hall, N.J., 1966).

### Paradise Lost

Leavis, F. R., *Revaluation*, 'Milton's Verse' (W. W. Norton & Co., New York, 1963).
Ricks, Christopher, *Milton's Grand Style* (Oxford Univ. Press, New York, 1963).
Lewis, C. S., Preface to *Paradise Lost* (Oxford Univ. Press, New York, 1942).
Waldock, A. J. A., *'Paradise Lost' and its Critics* (Cambridge Univ. Press, New York, 1947).
Broadbent, J. B., *Some Graver Subject* (Schocken Books, New York, 1967).

148

MacCaffrey, Isabel G., *'Paradise Lost' as Myth* (Harvard Univ. Press, Cambridge, Mass., 1959).

Cope, Jackson I., *Metaphoric Structure of 'Paradise Lost'* (John Hopkins Press, Baltimore, Md., 1962).

Empson, William, *Milton's God* (New Directions, New York, 1961).

Burden, Dennis, *The Logical Epic* (Harvard Univ. Press, Cambridge, Mass., 1967).

*Paradise Regained*

Pope, E. M., *'Paradise Regained': The Tradition and the Poem* (Russell & Russell, New York, 1947).

Lewalski, Barbara K., *Milton's Brief Epic* (Brown Univ. Press, Providence, R.I., 1966).

*Samson Agonistes*

Krouse, F. M., *Milton's Samson and the Christian Tradition,* (Princeton Univ. Press, Princeton, N.J., 1949).

Parker, W. R., *Milton's Debt to Greek Tragedy in 'Samson Agonistes'* (Barnes & Noble, New York, 1968).

# Index

## Stay On Top of Your Classwork with
## ARCO'S 1,000 IDEAS FOR TERM PAPER SERIES

Concise yet thorough guides to the planning and preparation of term papers for high school and college students—how to plan the paper, how and where to find research sources, how to organize the project, how to select a topic. $1.95 each, except where noted.

### 1,000 IDEAS FOR TERM PAPERS IN:

**AMERICAN HISTORY**
From pre-revolutionary times to the post-World War II period.

**ECONOMICS**
From macroeconomic theory to the literature of Smith, Marx, Keynes.

**ENGLISH**
From Chaucer to modern realism. **1.45**

**SOCIAL SCIENCE**
Topics on psychology, anthropology, sociology and political science.

**SOCIOLOGY**
Communications, war, urbanization, family, criminology, research design, analysis of data.

**WORLD LITERATURE**
From Beowulf to the twentieth century.

---

# Get More Mileage Out of Your Study Time!
## ARCO NOTES

An all-new series of study aids to help you get better grades in your lit courses. Each book gives chapter-by-chapter summaries, a brief general summary of the work, sketches of all major characters, a brief biography of the author, and an essential annotated bibliography. Use **Arco Notes**—they stick in your memory!                    95¢ each

THE AENEID
CRIME AND PUNISHMENT
DAVID COPPERFIELD
THE DIVINE COMEDY
GREAT EXPECTATIONS
HAMLET
THE HOUSE OF THE SEVEN GABLES
HUCKLEBERRY FINN
THE ILIAD
IVANHOE
JANE EYRE
JULIUS CAESAR
LEAVES OF GRASS
LORD JIM
MACBETH

MAN AND SUPERMAN
THE MERCHANT OF VENICE
MOBY DICK
MY ANTONIA
THE ODYSSEY
OTHELLO
PRIDE AND PREJUDICE
THE RED BADGE OF COURAGE
THE RETURN OF THE NATIVE
ROMEO AND JULIET
THE SCARLET LETTER
SILAS MARNER
A TALE OF TWO CITIES
THE TEMPEST
WUTHERING HEIGHTS